HANDBOOK for THEATRICAL APPRENTICES

A Practical Guide in All Phases of Theatre

By Dorothy Lee Tompkins

Copyright © 1962 by Samuel French, Inc.
Copyright © 1990 by Dorothy Dyas
ALL RIGHTS RESERVED

SAMUEL FRENCH, INC.
45 WEST 25TH STREET   NEW YORK 10010
7623 SUNSET BOULEVARD HOLLYWOOD 90046
LONDON   TORONTO

ABOUT THE AUTHOR

Dorothy Lee Tompkins is a veteran of twenty-three seasons of stock in addition to her university, community theatre, and Off-Broadway credits. She has played over two hundred roles and held just about every other job connected with the theatre. She received her degree from Ohio University and won a fellowship to study for her Master's degree. She is married to James Dyas, Producer-Director of the Red Barn Theatre in Saugatuck, Michigan. They have two children, Kathy and Jim-Billy.

PRINTED IN THE U. S. A.
0 573 69012

Table of Contents

	INTRODUCTION	5
1.	APPRENTICE	12
2.	AUTHOR	16
3.	BACKER	18
4.	BOX OFFICE STAFF	19
5.	BUSINESS MANAGER	23
6.	CAST	26
7.	CHOREOGRAPHER	37
8.	CHORUS	40
9.	CONCESSIONAIRE	41
10.	COSTUMIER	43
11.	CREW	52
12.	DIRECTOR	54
13.	DRESSER	66
14.	ELECTRICIAN	68
15.	JOBBER	74
16.	LIGHTING DESIGNER	78
17.	MAINTENANCE MAN	80
18.	MUSICAL DIRECTOR	86
19.	PATRON'S CHAIRMAN	89
20.	PHOTOGRAPHER	93
21.	PRODUCER	95
22.	PROPERTY MAN	111

Handbook for Theatrical Apprentices

23. PROPERTY MANAGER 119
24. PUBLICITY DIRECTOR 124
25. SCENE DESIGNER 135
26. SECRETARY 140
27. SOUND TECHNICIAN 143
28. STAGE MANAGER 150
29. STAR 161
30. TECHNICAL DIRECTOR 163
31. USHER 174
32. VARIETY WORKER 177
33. YOURSELF 179

Introduction

This book was written for apprentices in summer stock, students in drama schools, and new members of community theatre groups, but I harbor a sneaky suspicion that many a top-notch professional could take a peek at it occasionally (when the apprentices aren't looking, of course) without hurting his next production a bit. First, I want to make it absolutely clear that everything in this book has been said before. In fact, most of it has been said so often that it has practically become a round-robin conversation piece.

Summer stock personnel say it repeatedly from about the middle of June (when most summer stock seasons start) until about Thanksgiving. By Thanksgiving conversation about summer stock dies down a little because actors, scene designers, directors, stage managers, and anyone else connected with summer stock have usually spent their savings. They must, therefore, concentrate on new problems. The ones who are lucky, diligent, hardworking, just-right-for-a-part, lucky, at-the-right-place-at-the-right-time, competent, talented, healthy, and lucky can happily concentrate on a new production. Others must give their time and attention to finding a Christmas job—Macy's and the Post Office are big at Christmas time. Still others spend their time figuring out how they can send Christmas presents home, cards to their close friends and agents, and keep alive on unemployment insurance. All, even those who are working, must devote some attention to finding the next job in the theatre.

Meantime, however, community theatre members and drama students have taken up the recital. Their season lasts from about the middle of September until Memorial Day. Then of course come vacations, golf, swimming and other diversions which tend to blot out serious thoughts or discussions about last season's work.

Everyone in theatre, from stars to students, seems to remember only the good things about a closed show. No one forgets an applause exit, six personal curtain calls, or the red formal which caused three whistles, four ahs, and a light murmur throughout the house on a single entrance. These moments of pure delight inspire dreams of glory and autobiographies.

Oh, once in a while something really awful happens like the time (in the round) the leading man put his hand on a dowager's leg instead of the desk's during a blackout. Said dowager merely sat in stony silence when the lights came up. No one ever knew whether it was from joy or fear. That causes speculation.

Then, too, there was the time a little dog was sitting on the leading lady's lap, simply ruined her dress, you know, and she had to go to the bar and tie a bar towel around her middle to finish playing the scene. Or the times that electrical storms have blown the lights out all over town and entire shows have been played by candle and flashlight. These little tricks of fate, and worse, much worse, occur in the most able companies. They make pretty good stories and are bound to be repeated from time to time.

Really gigantic blunders make hilarious stories. Along about New Year's Eve, when theatre folk, like everybody else, relive the past year in a kind of little glow, they go over particularly well. The best ones are embellished and polished here and there (without distorting the truth, of course) and used again by actors when they are looking for work in summer stock or to impress a new community theatre director.

Small incompetences never make good stories. They are forgotten "between seasons." I suppose that is why no one else has ever written this book!

And so everything in this book continues to be said repeatedly season after season. In dressing rooms, green rooms, back stage, bars, class rooms, restaurants, drug stores, fancy hotel suites, dingy apartments, on the beach, or any place else where two or more theatre folk meet, the dialogue is likely to go something like this:

"How is the show going?" or "How was your season?" (according to the time of year). The answer: "Great, and would have been better, if only that damn-apprentice had . . . ." or "Terrible if only those damn-apprentices had . . . . , it would have been fine."

It is about those *dots* that I am writing this book. Sometimes the . . . . go on as long as an O'Neill speech and have just as much passion. In almost every instance "BEEN A PRO" could fill in the spaces nicely.

Let us stop here and now to define a professional, an amateur, an apprentice, a damn-apprentice, a pro, and an artist.

A professional stage manager, actor, scene designer, or whatever has had enough training and experience in his field to demand and get a salary.

An amateur or non-professional neither requests nor receives a salary for his theatrical work. He earns his living by being a doctor, lawyer, merchant, chief, or whatever, and he likes it. He has no desire to make the theatre a career. He enjoys giving his time and energy to the theatre or he wouldn't give it.

An apprentice usually has a large ambition and may have had some training and experience, but he is not yet skilled enough to be paid for his work.

The term, damn-apprentice, is used as often in the theatre as damn-yankee is used in the south. It can be applied to anyone connected with the theatre from the producer or star of the show to the local kid who kindly offers his services to pick up cigarette butts between the matinee and evening performances. A damn-apprentice is, then, any person who undertakes any job in the theatre and then does not do it.

A pro is one who always does his job. One of the highest compliments one theatrical person can pay another is to say, "He's pro." The lowest blasphemy that can be hurled is, "Well, he's just not pro."

An artist is a pro with magic.

This book will make no attempt to explain why some non-pros have highly paid positions while some really great artists become paupers. These phenomena are so mixed up with human emotions, abstractions, intangible factors, and business deals that I could never pretend to straighten them out. I leave that task to the psychiatrists and press agents.

I won't try to decipher terms like employment statistics, family wishes, comforts of home, and frogs in puddles, which always seem to creep into discussions about talented non-professionals who cling to amateur standing. I suggest that one of those pamphlets on vocations, avocations, and aptitude testing might supply an answer.

One question that is bound to come up is, "But how do I get a job in the theatre?" I don't know. Ask fifty people. Get fifty answers. By and large, I'd say, "One job leads to another," or "What you do in 1962 may get you a job in 1963—or even 1982." I may say, too, "There are forty-eight states in the union besides California and New York, if you really want to work." But all this belongs in another book called "Opportunities in Our Land," or some such title. No, alas, in these pages you will find no magic words telling you how to get a job in the theatre, movies, television, Mom and Pop's Cabaret, or any other phase of show business. I leave that to you, Lady Luck, and to your stage mother, if you have one.

I will also leave the do-it-yourself books on "How to Build a Flat," "How to Make a Costume," and "How to Analyze a Part," respectively and very respectfully to Your Stage Crew Handbook, The Singer Sewing Machine Company, and Stanislavsky.

I shall attempt three things.

1. To categorize the jobs in the living theatre. That isn't hard. Any theatre program from Broadway to Timbuktu has them all listed in black and white: Produced by, Directed by, Scenery designed by, Costumes by, etc.
2. To define these jobs and tell what basic responsibilities each job entails. The reader may add, subtract, multiply, or divide these duties according to the policies of the theatre where he is employed. They are fundamentally the same in any theatre—on a larger or smaller scale, with more or less assistants—depending on the size or financial status of the operation. In any case, the head of each department is responsible for the proper assignment, delineation and final execution of duties of his assistants.
3. To designate and clarify some simple rules for accomplishing these jobs.

I sincerely hope this book will help all beginners in the wonderful world of theatre to use their present knowledge more efficiently and thus conserve time and energy to learn more and more about their art.

I hope to help the, literally, thousands of people in the

United States today who are involved in productions of plays in the non-professional theatre. The term, "Non-professional," does not necessarily mean unprofessional. Many, many non-professional theatres in this country give excellent productions with talented performers in beautiful theatres, and operate at a profit. It means that all, or nearly all, of those connected with the productions work without pay, solely for the civic or cultural contribution they make to the community, or for the sheer excitement of theatre. The income made by the non-professional theatres goes toward defraying the expenses of the physical production, to compensating a professional staff director and occasionally a professional guest star. The remaining profit goes toward buying new equipment, improving the theatre, entertaining at cast parties, or contributing to local charities. The individual is not paid for his work in the non-professional theatre. He must organize his time to include his regular paying job and his theatre job for a given rehearsal period (ordinarily somewhere between three and six weeks). A non-professional theatre is usually called a Community, Civic, or Little Theatre. It includes the same jobs with the same definitions, the same duties, and the same rules for accomplishing them as any other theatre. Only the time element and the financial gain for the individual are different.

I also hope my book will be of service to the stock producers, staff members, community theatre directors, and drama faculties who must perpetually guide theatrical students through the routine and organizational tasks involved in all theatrical jobs.

I hope and believe that by pointing out some of those routine and organizational tasks I can steer some very talented and, yes, successful people away from the chaos sometimes referred to as ulcer gulch. Their creative ability may then be used to its fullest extent.

If I repeat myself, and I shall often, it is because I want each category to be clear within itself. The final chapter, *Yourself,* applies to everyone; therefore it need not be repeated in each category.

I also want it clearly understood that I am not discriminating against either sex. As far as I know, any theatrical work may be undertaken by either males or females. I simply don't want to write "or she" a thousand and one times, so I will always use "he."

In order to escape arguments about billing, and because I still haven't figured out whether the chicken or the egg comes first, the jobs in the living theatre will be discussed in alphabetical order.

And now as they say in dressing rooms, green rooms, backstage, or wherever-two-or-more-theatre-folk-get-together-at-about-nine-o'clock-when-dress-rehearsal-was-called-for-eight, "Why don't we get this show on the road?"

CHAPTER 1

Apprentice

An apprentice is a person who may have had some theatrical training, but is not yet skilled enough to be paid for his work. More often than not he is both young and ambitious. Apprentices are sometimes referred to as "slave labor." This unfortunate, unfair and, worst of all, inaccurate term causes many an apprentice to feel as "put upon" as Liza Doolittle did when she was forced to take a bath. Apprentices are not forced. They agree to trade their time and their work for practical experience in live theatre. Time can be defined as all there is, which is never quite enough. The apprentice's work is frequently the "dirty" or routine assignments.

Still it is a fair agreement. Students in universities, dramatic schools, and colleges must pay tuition unless they work their way through school; thus trading either time and work or money for training. It is the same for apprentices, except that they do not have the alternative of paying tuition. They must consent to work.

I dare say there are devious methods of by-passing this dirty work, provided the unskilled one has the ways and/or means. In this case he will certainly manage to get himself a more glorified title than "apprentice" and will not be dealt with here.

Obviously summer stock apprentices must be able to supply their own transportation costs and living expenses during the term of apprenticeship. The term of agreement for one season is usually from the beginning of rehearsals through the final "strike" night.

In no place else can a potential pro in the theatre cram so much experience into so short a time (due to such long hours, I suspect). In most instances he will be too busy to know how much he is learning during the course of the season. After it is all over and he is soaking in a nice, warm tub or lying on his long-neglected bed, some of his new-found knowledge can be sorted and filed away in his memory. When he gets into one of those conversations that begin, "How did your season go?" and he finds himself saying, "If only that damn apprentice had . . . . ," he can separate more wheat from the chaff. (One learns from both good and bad—what to do or what not to do, as the case may be.)

Only when his next show is in production can last season's apprentice really assemble his recently acquired information and skills—by using them. Even then, half the time he won't know where they came from. "Certain things, you *just know*," he says.

If I were allowed to give every apprentice only one piece of advice, it would be this: If you understand your assignment, begin immediately. If you are really baffled, never, oh, never say, "Oh, that's impossible," but, "What do you suggest I do first?" *Listen* to the answer and then Begin Immediately.

An apprentice's duty is usually to assist some member of the professional staff—i.e., assistant stage manager, assistant costumer, assistant prop man, assistant in the box-office, etc., etc., etc. Many of the tasks listed and defined in the following chapters will never be left to the apprentice while he is an apprentice. Half a dozen "for Examples" selected at random are:

1 CHAPTER 5—*Item 4*

   The Business Manager must . . . pay all bills when they are due.

2 CHAPTER 12—*Item 1*

   The Director must . . . select the play or agree to producer's selection.

3 CHAPTER 15—*Item 1B*

   A Professional Jobber in summer stock is usually hired to . . . make up the Equity quota of union members needed in large cast shows.

4 CHAPTER 8—*Item 5*

   The Musical Director must . . . set keys for performers at earliest possible moment.

5 CHAPTER 24—*Item 3B*

   The Publicity Director must . . . plan to spend about ten percent of the possible gross on advertising.

   CHAPTER 25—*Item 2*

   The Scene Designer must . . . determine his budget.

Of course, there are many others. I have tried to include most of the basic inner workings of a whole theatre operation in order to show the apprentice:

1 What he should be able to expect from seasoned staff members;
2 Some of the jobs he may be able to "take over," thus freeing his department head for more skillful or creative work;
3 At least some of the reasons for his assignments;
4 What he must be able to expect from himself before he is ready to leave the ranks of apprentices.

Except to say that an apprentice must work and learn by assisting a regular staff member, I have shown no special duties for him. I can only say that I believe each apprentice should have as many kinds of jobs as possible during his first year of apprenticeship, and that he should do each one to the best of his ability. By the second year, particularly if he goes back with the same company, he may be able to escape some of the jobs he does not like.

Due to the fact that most apprentices know very little about the inner workings of the theatre, most of them want to be actors . . . almost to a man. Therefore it seems only fair to include a special note on acting. When an apprentice is assigned a part, he is expected to conduct himself as a regular member of the cast during rehearsals and performance (see Chapter 6, THE CAST); *and* he is also expected to carry on with one of his assisting jobs as well. Even stars of tomorrow or last night are not exempt!

The best way to be of assistance is to *know* what the job entails and then to *do* everything possible toward seeing that the job is done.

CHAPTER 2

Author

An author is a person who has written a play.

By the time his play reaches summer stock or community theatre production, he has usually turned it over to Samuel French, Brandt & Brandt, or some other reputable play service. His only job now is to wait for his royalty check to arrive and, we hope, write another play.

Once in a while, however, a theatre manager finds a new play and wants to try it out. If the author agrees to this he should:

1 Make sure that the producer has at least three copies of the play before the season begins.

    A—One for the typist to make sides.

    B—One for the director and stage manager.

    C—One for the scene designer.

2 Arrive on the scene before the first rehearsal.

    A—Some misunderstandings are inevitable in an unproduced play. The author may be able to untangle some of them with the director, producer, and scene designer before the cast and crew become involved, thus saving untold wear and tear on temperament.

    B—He may see "his" actors in a finished production and thus have some idea of their work. This may keep him from pressing the panic button during the fumble-fumble

Handbook for Theatrical Apprentices

stage of rehearsal. He can also note that his leading lady looks pretty good when she is all curled and girdled even if she looks like an egg on a potato sack in her pin curlers and slacks.

3 Not interrupt rehearsals.
4 Never undermine the authority of the director.
    A—A house divided against itself . . . .
    B—It confuses actors to be given directions, interpretations, etc., by several people.
    C—If the author's ideas will play, most directors welcome them, IF they are given through the director.
5 Always bring a notebook or clip board and several sharpened pencils to rehearsals.
6 Have access to a typewriter and/or a typist.
7 Rewrite scenes that need revision and have them ready for the actors as soon as humanly possible.
8 Watch the play in performance. Make additional notes.
9 Change the things that can be changed effectively, with the director's approval, and in the time allowed.
10 Save the rest of the notes for future re-writing.
11 Make no verbal agreements that anyone connected with the production will be involved in it when it reaches Broadway, unless he is absolutely positive that he has the power to carry out this agreement. (I trust that he will have the good sense not to put anything in writing, except the new scenes for his play.)

CHAPTER 3

The Backer

The backer is a person who invests money in the theatre. He must:
1. Have money.
2. Have knowledge of tax laws governing theatrical investments or:
3. Have a business manager who knows them.
4. Decide upon a producer or group with whom to invest.
5. Decide how much money he is ready, willing, and able to invest.
6. Invest the money through proper legal procedure.
7. Agree that the producer is to use the money as he sees fit.

NOTE: If the backer insists upon, or agrees to accept for any reason, any further authority concerning the operation of the theatre, he automatically becomes a co-, assistant-, or full-fledged producer. Chapter 22 deals with the duties and problems of the PRODUCER.

FURTHER NOTE: The potential backer may be wise to have at least a fleeting knowledge of Chapter 22 before he follows through with "4," "5," "6" and "7" of the above.

CHAPTER 4

Box Office Staff

The box office staff includes the people who make reservations and sell tickets for current and future performances. They should always:

1. Be on time.
2. Make sure the box office is clean and neat at all times whether there is a janitor to do the scrubbing and polishing or not.
3. Have a reservation book with its own pencil tied, nailed, or glued to its most convenient spot.
4. Never lend the above except on police order or when it is a matter of life and death—really.
5. Have personal notebook and pencils for special notes, grocery lists, and doodling.
6. Make sure a seating chart is in full view—both for ticket buyer and box office personnel.
7. Memorize the price scale and the schedule of plays.
8. Have both in full view anyway in case of memory lapse.
9. Rack up tickets as far in advance as equipment allows.
10. Request more racks if they are needed. (If this fails, demand them; if this fails, build them; if this fails, resign.)
11. Have two files.

  A—A daily file for the current show.
  B—A weekly file for future productions.
12 Keep change available at all times.
13 Learn to make change quickly and correctly.
14 Always state the name of the theatre and ask, "May I help you?" when answering the phone.
15 Always speak clearly.
16 Always be courteous. Never forget the magic words, "please" and "thank you."
17 Be friendly to customers and potential customers. It helps to remember names of "regulars."
18 Be able to give clear-cut directions to the theatre by all modes of transportation.
19 Be able to discuss the current play intelligently, at least to the extent of knowing the title, the author, type of play, and the leading players.
20 Write ticket reservations in the reservation book as they are being made.
  A—Name of person.
  B—Date. State whether it is for matinee or evening.
  C—Number of reservations.
  D—Row and number of seats requested. Never promise or even indicate that certain seats are available without checking.
  E—The price of each ticket.
  F—Total amount to be collected.
  G—If patron or season or complimentary ticket is being used, that information may replace ticket prices.
21 Pull tickets immediately after reservations are made.
22 Mark ticket envelopes clearly.
  A—Name (must be marked immediately!)
  B—Date.

Handbook for Theatrical Apprentices   21

    C—Number of reservations.
    D—Seats, by row and number.
    E—Price of each ticket.
    F—Total amount to be collected.
    G—If patron, season or complimentary ticket is being used, that information may replace ticket prices. Note: If phone is jangling and box office is busy, B through G may be postponed until there is a lull, *provided ALL of 20, 21, and A of 22 have been accurately accomplished, and a special place has been provided for unfinished envelopes.*
23 Place completed ticket envelopes in correct file immediately.
24 Keep current files up to date.
25 Check regularly to see that information on reservation book and ticket envelopes coincide.
26 Count the money and the ticket stubs at the end of each evening and balance the books. NOTE: This is usually done with the business manager.
27 Either deposit the cash each evening or turn it over to the business manager according to the policy of the theatre.
28 Place ticket stubs and unused tickets in a sealed, dated envelope and retain for tax purposes.
29 Never, never, never leave the tickets or the money unattended.
30 If the box office phone is the only available phone, the box office staff must, unfortunately, take personal calls on it. They should, however:
    A—Avoid lengthy conversations during working hours.
    B—Avoid interrupting rehearsals by saying,

"He's in rehearsal right now. May I take your number and have him call you?"

C—If this doesn't work, ask the director or stage manager if Mr. So-and-So may come to the phone, or find out when he may be reached.

D—Make sure that anybody who makes a personal call finds out the charges and writes them in a book provided for this purpose—before he leaves the box office.

31 Dress neatly.

32 Remember that old adage learned at mother's knee: "Politeness is to do and say the kindest thing in the kindest way."

CHAPTER 5

Business Manager

The business manager is the person who controls the money. He must:
1. Make and/or approve the budget. (See Section 3 Chapter 21.)
2. See that the staff stays within that budget.
    A—Designate a certain time each week for all department heads to turn in expense accounts for a particular show.
    B—Set up charge accounts in certain stores and make it clear to all members of the staff that they can charge items in those stores only.
    C—Make it clear to stores that bills will be paid by the theatre only when specific people sign for goods received. (In case of emergency, i.e., when another person must be sent for goods, he must carry a note signed by a department head.)
    D—Inform department heads immediately, when they exceed the budget.
3. Request that all creditors send bills to the theatre to the attention of the business manager.
4. Pay all bills when they are due (or kindly placate the creditors until this is possible).
5. Know all the union rulings. Keep a rule book handy anyway in case memory lapses or petty details crop up.

6 See that all contracts are promptly and legally signed. In the case of professional actors:
   - A—Mail green copy of every contract to Actor's Equity immediately.
   - B—File one white copy of every contract immediately.
7 Have employees fill out Employees Withholding Exemption Certificates immediately. File.
8 Make typewritten copies of names and permanent addresses of employees. File.
9 Pay professional actors on time. (They can never be placated.)
10 Pay professional staff members on time.
11 Order scripts and sides in plenty of time.
   - A—Two weeks before rehearsal date is usually sufficient.
   - B—Make sure royalty check is enclosed with order.
12 Check box office receipts each night.
   - A—See that ticket stubs and cash balance.
   - B—Keep unused tickets and ticket stubs in specified place (for tax purposes).
   - C—Make arrangements for nightly deposit. Business manager may do this himself or give responsibility to one member of the box office staff.
   - D—Keep daily accounts of other monies received.
13 Keep weekly books, giving a "by the show" account of income and liabilities. (Heaven will bless all good accountants.)
14 Make a final set of books at the end of the season, giving a complete report on all income and liabilities. (Heaven will *surely* bless all good accountants.)

15 Make an improved budget at the end of the season for the following season based on the final report.
16 Make sure all files are in order at the end of the season.
17 Make arrangements for outlying and out-of-season bills to be paid.
   - A—Leave forwarding address so that mail may be forwarded, or make arrangements to pick up mail at regular intervals.
   - B—Either continue to pay bills regularly during the off seasons, or turn complete responsibility, including all books, over to management before leaving the company.
   - C—Never, never, never just decide between seasons that he can't be bothered any more. (More lawsuits have been caused that way.)
   - D—Send back employers reports on professional actors and staff members to unemployment offices immediately. (Actors and other employees consider this as part of their due and, I repeat, they cannot be placated.)
18 Become familiar with tax laws in his particular locale.
19 During the entire season get everything in writing. (It isn't that a business manager doesn't trust everyone, but he has his duties and his right.)
20 Send W-2 forms to all professional employees as soon after the close of the season as possible. *Never* later than the following January 1.

CHAPTER 6

The Cast

The cast includes everyone who appears in a play.

Volumes have been written on the art of acting. Theories run rampant. They are as numerous as equity cards and even "numerouser." I do not propose to dispute any of them. Every theory is a good one if it works for the performer who uses it. I believe the following rules will be adaptable to any theory. I know they will give the performer in summer stock and in community theatre a fighting chance to give a polished performance. They are based on the pre-conceived notion that an actor must say, do, and wear *something*.

1 The actor must say something.

    A—Learn his "words" promptly. An act a day is a reasonable goal in stock. There are many excuses for failure to memorize words. There is only one reason—the actor has not studied them sufficiently. Everyone has different rates of speed for learning. Most actors find it helpful to study aloud, thus letting the mouth as well as the mind become familiar with the words.

    B—Learn his lines as they are written. Usually the author has written and rewritten them in order to achieve a certain effect. If the actor changes them haphazardly they will probably lose some of the effect even if the actual meaning remains the same.

C—Let the stage manager know if the lines have been changed purposely. I can think of only four valid reasons.

(1) The actor may have a speech impediment which makes it impossible for him to say certain words correctly.

(2) The lines may refer to props or characters in a way that will not fit a particular production.

For example: The line may be—"What lovely red velvet drapes." If the drapes are to be green brocade, the line must obviously be changed. Or the line may read, "The girl of my dreams is a tall, slender blonde." The plot will plainly thicken if the girl is a plump brunette. Still it is wise to check before changing the line. Many a girl has rehearsed with raven tresses only to become a honey blonde by opening night.

(3) The play may be too long. In this instance the director will usually do the cutting. The actor may suggest cuts in his own part (what am I saying?), but they must be cleared with the director, stage manager, and author if he is available.

(4) Certain words are taboo in certain areas. (That, unfortunately, is *that*.)

D—Ask the stage manager for a line if he forgets it in rehearsal.

(1) Never snap his fingers or whistle for a line to be thrown—unless, of course, the stage manager is a dog.

(2) Never apologize or give excuses for not knowing lines. This wastes valuable

time. If the actor knows the line, he will say it on stage. If not, nobody, but nobody, cares why or where he may have known it.

E—Never ask for a line during performance or dress rehearsal. By this time an actor should know the play well enough to "cover," i.e., say or do something that will keep the play going until he or someone else can pick up the dialogue.

F—Say his lines so that they can be heard. (Otherwise, they simply aren't any good to anybody.)

G—Pick up his cues. Moments of silence can be most effective, but these moments must be built for and filled with something. A pause is pregnant. A stage wait is merely bloated.

2 Do something.

A—Be on time for rehearsals and listen to his own entrance cues. The stage manager or assistant cannot be dashing about looking for actors. Apprentices who have other jobs to do may not be allowed to sit through full rehearsals. It is all the more important for them to find out when they enter, learn a warn cue, and be there at the approximated time unless they are given specific orders by the stage manager to do otherwise. No member of the cast should ever leave the premises without permission from the stage manager.

NOTE: Permission from the technical director, the backer's wife, or the prettiest apprentice doesn't count!

B—*Listen* when the stage manager, director, or scene designer explains the set. Otherwise, it is very difficult to tell which folding chair is the grand piano and which is grandfather's portrait.

C—Whenever possible, find out which way doors will open and close, whether the easy chair will have arms, how much of the stairway will be visible, etc.

D—Learn his business, i.e., where he is to go and what he is to do when he gets there.

(1) Write his business in the sides (lightly) as it is given by the director, so that it can be visualized as he learns his lines.

(2) Try the business when the director gives it to him.

(3) Ask the director to change business if it remains uncomfortable after several tries. No fair cheating. A better suggestion is usually welcome!

(4) Never be afraid to add bits and pieces on his own if they add to the general scheme of the production.

(5) Never be obstinate about taking out beloved bits if they detract from the play. (Remember them though; they may be just the thing for another production.)

E—Handle props easily.

(1) Rehearse with makeshift hand props as soon as he gets the book out of his hands.

(2) Make his own prop list.

(3) Rehearse with correct props as soon as they are available for use.

(4) Always, always, always check his props before run-throughs or performances. (No matter who is to blame for a missing prop, the actor is the one who is left floundering.)

F—Be on time for performance.
> (1) Half hour before curtain is the accepted rule; however, if the actor's makeup and other preparations take longer, he should give himself ample time.
>
> (2) If the actor does not appear until the second or third act he may get permission from the stage manager to arrive later than half hour. He must never arrive later without such permission.
>
> (3) As for missing or being late for an entrance, may God forgive him; no one else will.

G—Never steal a scene.

NOTE: This does not mean that any actor should be dull, or that he shouldn't put up a legitimate fight for special attention in a scene which is his by rights. It doesn't even mean that the star, the director, or the author won't give a scene to a bit player. It simply means that *an ostentatious display of unnecessary gyrations,* which detract from the play as a whole, is not only imprudent but the distinct mark of a ham.

Stealing is taboo in our society. A thief is a thief whether he practices in the five and dime, The Federal Bank of America, or on stage.

H—Make no unnecessary noise backstage.
> This needs no further comment. Noise is a curse whether it be made with the mouth, the feet, or slippery hand props. Even a "growling tummy" is frowned upon.
>
> This rule goes into effect at least by half hour and continues until the audience has made its final exit.

I—Take curtain calls graciously.
> (1) They are part of the performance if not the play.

(2) Small parts who go on before the leads should move quickly and quietly.

(3) If small parts are to exit before the leads enter, they should move quickly and quietly.

(4) If they are to re-enter they should move quickly and quietly.

(5) After the final *rehearsed* call, no one should leave his position until he is dismissed by the stage manager.

J—Always check the call board before he leaves the theatre. (Who knows, he may miss a rehearsal, a union meeting, or a lovely party.)

3 Wear something.

A—Determine how many and what kind of costumes his part involves.

(1) Check through his own wardrobe to find out which of these he can furnish himself. Show them to the costumier.

(2) Report his other needs to costumier immediately. It is best to do this in writing. (If an actor passes a costumier on the stairs and says, "Look honey, I want a red tie, some blue pants, and a diamond stick pin," the costumier may think he is mentally composing a letter to Santa Claus.)

(3) Let the costumier know where the missing costumes can be obtained if he has the information, but has no time to get the costume himself.

(4) Make sure the costumier has his measurements and sizes.

(5) Have costumes fitted as soon as they are available.

B—Rehearse at least part of the time in a reasonable facimile of his costumes—even though he doesn't wear the ones he will use in performance.

For example: The actor should get used to wearing a coat if he is to put in on, take it off, or take something out of his pocket during performance. An actress can do business in slacks or shorts that she can't even consider doing in a tight skirt. (A note in passing: I shudder to think of the number of times I have heard directors give this note after dress rehearsal, "Please don't sit on your tails.")

C—Rehearse at least part of the time in the shoes he will wear in performance. This applies particularly to women, because they just do walk differently in three-inch heels than they do in flats. Men may run into problems with cowboy boots, sneakers, elevateds, etc., so I think it is a worthwhile consideration for them too.

D—Make sure his costumes are clean, pressed, in good repair, and complete for every performance including dress rehearsals.

NOTE: Frequently the costumier and assistants take care of this if the costumes are marked and put in the designated place. If such service is unavailable, the actor must do it himself or ask a friend to do it. In any case, it is his own responsibility until his eminence, and consequently salary, make a personal valet possible. (Possession of an Equity Card does not automatically entitle an actor to valet service from stock apprentices.)

E—Always return costumes to dressing room after performance.

F—Remove "has been" costumes from dressing room on closing night.

    (1) Leave personal costumes which must be cleaned by management in designated place.

    (2) Return personally borrowed costumes to rightful owners after necessary cleaning and repairs.

    (3) Return rented and other borrowed costumes to costumier. (If these need repairs, notify costumier by pinning a note to the costume.)

    (4) Take personal items home so they won't be "returned" to somebody.

NOTE: Costumier may prefer that these costumes be left in the dressing room for removal.

FINAL NOTE TO PROFESSIONALS: An actor who constantly "throws the book" at the management on other rules should remember that "the book" clearly states that actors must furnish their own modern wardrobe.

G—Furnish his own make-up.

    (1) Each will need:
        Cold cream.
        Tissue.
        A light base.
        A dark base.
        A light powder.
        A dark powder.
        A light creme rouge.
        A dark creme rouge.
        A lipstick brush.
        Eyeshadow (his own color).
        Mascara (particularly if he is fair).
        Hair brush and comb.
        Clothes brush.

Pins, needles, scissors, light and dark thread.

Nail file and/or nail cutter.

Shoe polish and shoe brush.

(2) He may need:

Body make-up.

Hair whitener or white shoe polish.

Silver spray.

A brown liner.

(3) An actress will need:

Several shades of lipstick (her own colors will probably suffice).

(4) An actress should be well supplied with:

All sorts of hair paraphernalia—hair pins, bobby pins, hair nets, combs, barrettes, curlers, hairspray.

(5) An actress with short hair may need:

Hair pieces or switches in her own color (particularly if period plays are scheduled).

NOTE: The dime store variety are good enough for stage purposes, and, if cared for properly, are a good long-range investment.

(6) An actor may need:

Spirit gum.

Crepe hair in his own color (particularly if period plays are scheduled).

(7) An actor or actress who is starting a new make-up kit should *not* invest in:

Dozens of shades of base, powder, rouge, liner, eyeshadow, crepe hair, *or* specialized supplies such as nose putty, tooth black (even if they do sound like fun).

H—Apply his own make-up.

(1) The actor should always apply make-up for dress rehearsal so it can be checked by the director:

(a) Under lights.

(b) With costumes.

(c) In comparison with other performers.

(2) He should change his make-up in accordance with notes given by the director (after the first act if possible (so new make-up can be checked.

(3) Try new make-up for final run-through if his has been unsatisfactory, whether all performers are required to use make-up or not.

(4) He must pay careful attention to his application of make-up so he can repeat it exactly for each performance.

NOTE: An actor who has a touch of gray in his hair for opening night is not easily forgiven if he looks as if he fell into a flour barrel by mid-week.

(5) He should apply character or age lines sparingly, if at all, and blend carefully.

NOTE: Definite lines all over his face may make him look like a zebra in costume. Smudgy lines may make him look like a dirty little boy. Most likely, either one will merely serve to make him look like himself with lines drawn on his face. 'Tis most distracting.

(6) He should experiment with his make-up several days before dress rehearsal if it is to be an odd or unusual one for him.

(a) It may help him to arrive at a better characterization.

(b) It will help him to arrive at a satisfactory make-up for his present role.

(c) It will help him to find out things about his own facial structure and the use of make-up for future roles.

(7) He should ask a more experienced person if he does not know how to apply his own make-up.

NOTE: For heaven's sake, never wait until half-hour on dress rehearsal to do it.

(8) He must remember that hair-dos (for both men and women) and posture are as important to a good make-up as any amount of "goo" that he can smear on his face. There is no point in asking anyone to check one without the other.

(9) The actor must take the director's word for it if he says make-up is unsatisfactory.

NOTE: The simple fact is—make-up just does look different under lights and at a distance. The director can see it; the actor cannot.

I—Keep his own dressing-table reasonably neat and clean. It is his home for the duration of the play.

CHAPTER 7

The Choreographer

The choreographer is the person who designs and teaches the dances. The choreographer should:
1. Know the music.
2. Determine the size of the stage area to be used.
3. Determine approximately how much training and/or ability his dancers have—as far in advance as possible.
    - A—Sometimes the choreographer is permitted to audition and hire many professional dancers.
    - B—Sometimes he must "take what comes" from apprentices, near-by dancing students, and local housewives. (Tact is of the essence here.)
    - C—Sometimes he may have a combination of both.
4. Determine, with costumier's approval, the general style of costumes to be worn.
5. Take 1, 2, 3, and 4 into consideration when designing dances. No wishful thinking allowed.
6. Design the dances in advance and write them down.
    - A—Accept the fact that there will be precious little time for "on the floor" creation.
    - B—Make changes only when absolutely necessary.

7 Never waste rehearsal time.
- A—Begin rehearsals on time, i.e., have rehearsal clothes on, stage set, music ready, warm-up exercises taken, coffee consumed, etc., before rehearsals are scheduled to start.
- B—Determine how much rehearsal time each dance should need and schedule rehearsals accordingly.
- C—Settle rehearsal schedules for principals with director.
- D—Settle fitting schedules with costumier.
- E—Make schedule changes only when absolutely necessary.
- F—Post rehearsal schedules.
- G—Explain "A" to each person as he is accepted as a member of the chorus.
- H—Reiterate "A" at the first rehearsal call.
- I—Post Rule "A" along with rehearsal schedule.
- J—Command discipline during rehearsals.

  (1) Remember that excess discussion of a dance is useless. The dancer's body, as well as his mind, must know the dances. The more often he actually *does* the dances in rehearsal the more likely he is to perform them correctly.

  (2) Make as few changes in each dance as possible.

  (3) GIVE DIRECTIONS CLEARLY BOTH TO REHEARSAL PIANIST AND TO DANCERS.

  (4) Demand that his dancers give complete co-operation to the director when the show is put together.

K—Follow the rules for "the cast" (pp. 26) if he is to appear in the show. Actually, a choreographer who is to perform also should prepare his own dances before regular rehearsals start. He will probably find barely enough time and energy for brush-up rehearsals.

CHAPTER 8

The Chorus

The chorus is that part of the cast who performs as a group. Each member of the chorus must
1. Remember that he is a member of the cast and follow the rules for "the cast." (See Chapter 6.)
2. Perform in exact unison with his group if that be a requirement.
3. Pay special attention to the rule—Never steal a scene. (See Section "2-G" in Chapter 6.)

CHAPTER 9

The Concessionaire

The concessionaire is the person who runs the refreshment stand.

He may rent the space and run his concession as a separate business, or he may run the stand for the management. It either case his business is part and parcel of the entire theatre operation and deserves space in a book of this kind. The concessionaire should:

1 Keep his shop clean and in order.
2 Always appear neat and clean himself.
3 See that his stand is well stocked at every performance.
   A—Make original order far enough in advance for all items to be delivered before the theatre opens.
   B—Check delivery dates of all companies.
   C—Constantly check items sold and re-order diminishing items far enough in advance to have them delivered before he runs out.
   D—Never give an unauthorized person the key to the stock room.
4 Keep account of all bills.
   A—Pay the bills on time—if he is running his own business or:
   B—Turn the bills over to the business manager weekly—if he is running the stand for the management.

C—Keep his own set of books in either instance.
5 Be ready to open his stand on time.
   A—Have soft drinks cold.
   B—Have coffee hot, cream and sugar out.
   C—Have paper cups ready.
   D—Have candy, gum, cigarettes, etc. on display.
   E—Have plenty of change available.
6 Prepare for each intermission as soon as the curtain goes up.
7 Serve quickly.
8 Make change quickly and accurately.
9 Remember the magic words—"please" and "thank you."
10 Be quiet during performance.
11 Never leave the stand unattended.
12 Never leave the till unattended!
13 Count the money at the end of each performance. (Give his figures to the business manager at regular intervals—if he runs stand for management.)
14 See that money is locked up, deposited, or turned over to business manager at the end of each performance.
15 Make sure unused items are picked up and paid for or deducted from final bill at the end of the season.
16 Make a final and complete itemized financial report at the end of the season.
17 Turn above report over to business manager (unless concession is a separate business).
18 Return keys to management at the end of the season.

CHAPTER 10

The Costumier

The costumier is the person responsible for costumes.

He may have a wardrobe mistress and seamstresses to help him but chances are he won't. Even so, the costumier should use his time to organize the costumes, console the actors (they always need a lot of that), and do the things that no one else can do. If he does not have regular assistants he cannot demand help, but he can get it. "Ask and ye shall receive" almost always works.

Bit players and choruses are usually more than willing to help in their free time, *if* they know what needs to be done. On big shows let it be known that help is needed. Almost anyone can sew on a snap or turn up a hem. Some can even make a whole costume! When someone asks, "Is there anything I can do?" never hem and haw. Answer quickly, "Why you wonderful thing, of course!" Be ready to hand over a specific task then and there.

The costumier must remember that almost every actor has one of two terrible faults. He either thinks, "Mine are the only *important* costumes in the show," or "It doesn't matter what I *wear*." There seems to be no happy medium. Anyway, both are plainly wrong, but neither will ever be convinced. The only solution is to smile indulgently and be kind but firm about fittings.

The work involved, particularly in large cast and/or period productions, requires Herculean strength coupled with the patience of Job—and pure unadulterated organization. However, most schedules include plays with simple modern wardrobe requirements. For these plays, most actors furnish most of their own clothes, thus deleting about nine-tenths of the costumier's duties. They are relatively easy weeks.

With all of the above in mind, the costumier should divide his innumerable tasks into seven classifications and *work as far ahead as possible, and stay within his budget.*

The costumier must:

1 Determine the kind, number, and sizes of costumes needed. In order to do this he should:

A—Read the play. 'Tis a wise person who reads the plays before the beginning of the season. Impractical as it may seem, for stock only one master script is sent along with the sides. By the time the director, scene designer and stage manager have finished passing it frantically back and forth, the poor costumier has started on his *second* classification or he cannot possibly be ready for opening. Blessed be the publishing companies who include a costume plot in the back of the script. (I understand that this is the doing of the original stage manager. If so, bless him too!) "Costume plots" cannot be followed exactly, but if they say, "Louise, Act I, Sc. 1—Pale green chiffon afternoon dress, pink satin shoes, pink satin bag, pink satin sash, white straw hat with pink satin roses, white kidskin gloves," the costumier can be reasonably sure that the first scene takes place in the summer, there is a character named Louise, and she appears in the first act fairly dressed up. Then, even if he has no idea what Louise has to do with the play, whether she is 16 or 60, or indeed knows nothing more about her (except that she was originally played by someone who wore pink and green), he can begin.

B—Make a written costume plot listing all neccessary costumes for each performer. For example: Louise, Act I, Sc. 1, Dressy dress, shoes, hat, bag, gloves.

C—Post the basic costume plot on the first day of rehearsal—never later than the second; or schedule short conferences with each actor (one member of a chorus is usually sufficient) on the first or second day of rehearsal.

D—Add colors, materials, etc., to basic costume plot as they are determined.

For example: Dressy blue satin dress (long), blue satin shoes and bag, white flower hat, white gloves.

E—Keep one copy of the costume plot. One never knows when one will do the play again; besides, the posted one may be marked, or even torn up before costumes can be returned.

F—Have at least one book showing period costumes.

G—Check with scene designer regarding colors before buying, making, renting or approving costumes.

H—Keep file cards stating sizes and measurements of each actor.

I—Post the following rules for performers at the beginning of the season (particularly useful in resident companies).

COSTUME RULES FOR PERFORMERS

1. The costumier will assume that the actor expects to be responsible for all of his own modern wardrobe unless otherwise noted on the costume plot by noon of the third day of rehearsal. Sooner will be duly appreciated.
2. Each actor must bring his own things to the costumier by noon of the third day of rehearsal if he expects any work to be done on them. Sooner will be duly appreciated.
3. Actors will please check out costumes before half hour of dress rehearsal.
4. Actors must check their own costumes at the end of each performance, tag them for repairs, laundry, or pressing, and hang them on the rack provided for that purpose *before* leaving the theatre, or the costumier cannot be responsible for their condition.
5. Actors must polish their own shoes.
6. Actors must place cleaning on rack provided for that purpose on closing night of each production or costumier will not be responsible for cleaning.
7. Resident actors may arrange to have all cleaning done at the end of the season if they so desire.
8. Costumier will try to obtain costumes in time for correct fittings and alterations. Actors must, however, furnish the body to be fitted.
9. Any performer who chooses to keep his own wardrobe trim and neat will not lose prestige or cause hurt feelings to anyone in the costume department.
10. Actors must return borrowed or rented costumes to costumier on each closing night.

               Thank you for your co-operation.

2. Determine where and how the costumes may be obtained.

- A—Make use of actor's own wardrobe whenever possible, thus saving errand and alteration time.
- B—Use available theatre-owned costumes. The costumier should become familiar with the company wardrobe early in the season.
- C—Borrow from local people. The practiced costumier has an eye for clothes and sizes at receptions, intermissions, in shops, and even while innocently walking down the street.
- D—Rent costumes. Local community theatres are frequently well-stocked and inexpensive. Local costume companies may be cheaper and faster than the larger houses. If costumes must be *ordered* make sure the order is absolutely clear as to size, type of costume, and color.
- E—Design and build costumes from available material. Many a stunning costume has been made from old drapes, no longer fashionable evening dresses, etc. Imaginatiton is of the essence, but then so is time.
- F—Buy costumes or parts of costumes. Consider long term value.
- G—Design and build costumes from new material. Sometimes this is actually cheaper in the long run (and certainly more exciting) than renting costumes. Consider the time as well as the money involved, however.
- H—*List all items needed.*

3 Somehow get the costumes and keep records of where they were obtained and how much they cost.

- A—Gather actor's own costumes on a rack *or*

approve them and ask actor to bring them again for dress rehearsal.

B—Gather theatre costumes on a rack.

C—Make every trip count. Phone ahead if advisable. When going for borrowed or rented costumes and/or new materials and equipment, pick up *everything* that is to be obtained in that area.

D—Keep all receipts and note all miscellaneous expenditures such as phone calls, parking meters, etc., in a little black book.

E—Keep own address book denoting name, address, and phone number of everyone lending costumes.

F—If lenders want program credit, be sure to get correct wording and turn it over to publicity director promptly.

4 Fit the costumes and make necessary alterations.

A—Keep costume room or work space in reasonable order.

B—Always have equipment ready for use, i.e., sewing machine, iron, ironing board, needles, thread, zippers, hooks and eyes, snaps, elastic, pins, trimming, tailor's chalk.

C—Fit each costume as soon as it is obtained—rehearsal schedule permitting. (Costumier may have to be a wee bit stern.)

D—Mark each costume for alterations at fitting. Pin a tag to the costume with instructions, e.g., actor's name, dye green, hook and eye, waist at pin, lace edge on collar as pinned, press. Write same instructions on costume plot.

E—Hang tagged costumes in separate place.

F—Alter costumes as soon after fitting as superhumanly possible.

G—Apply above rule to building new costumes.

H—Apply above rule to dying costumes (except when several items are to be dyed the same color; then wait for all to be ready for the dye pot.)

I—Cross instructions off name tag and costume plot as each task is completed. (Imagine six people shortening the same trousers one inch.)

J—When costume is completed, hang it on a separate rack. Leave name tag on it.

K—Remember that all costumes *should* be pressed by dress rehearsal, and *must* be pressed by opening night. Costumier will simply have to use his own judgment as to which costumes need pressing and which do not, and when pressing can be done most effectively.

There is no point in wasting hours pressing clothes that will be mussed up in tech rehearsal. On the other hand all pressing can never be completed between tech and dress rehearsals. If pressing is put off too long, having costumes ready for opening night will be a push.

L—Make notes at dress rehearsals for corrections and additions.

M—Decide which corrections and/or additions are most important, and do first things first.

5 Keep costumes in good condition through run of the show.

A—Ask actors or stage manager if help is needed for fast costume changes.

B—Ask actors or dressers to hang costumes up after each change. (They should know this!)

C—Ask actors to put tags on costumes which need repair, laundry, or pressing *before* leaving theatre after each performance.

D—Stress the fact that names must be on tags.

E—Set aside a part of each day for laundry, repairs, and pressing. Laundry should be done early.

F—Hang costumes back on rack before half hour.

6 Return costumes promptly when show closes.

A—Sort costumes and mark for returning on strike night.

B—Have borrowed costumes cleaned—and repaired if necessary. It just isn't nice to take torn or dirty costumes back to their rightful owners. Besides they may be needed again.

C—See that actors' wardrobes are sent to cleaners.

D—Pack rented costumes and take them or send them back immediately. Make sure every piece of each rented costume is accounted for; costume houses can get very nasty about one missing spat.

E—Put theatre wardrobe in proper place on strike night or next morning. If they are too soiled to be used again, have them cleaned *before* putting them away.

F—Ask actors to remove their personal clothing from dressing rooms on each closing night. (It won't do much good, but it's a worthy request.)

G—Note when costumes are returned—and to

whom. One week should be ample time for cleaning, etc.

H—Give weekly itemized account to business manager.

7 Close up shop at the end of the season. If everything has been done correctly during the season, all the costumier has to do is:

A—Make a final check to see that everything has been returned.

B—Write thank-you notes to those who have been helpful. (Not necessary, but very much appreciated.)

C—Put moth balls in theatre owned costumes.

D—Add up his accounts and turn them over to business manager.

E—Return keys to management.

CHAPTER 11

The Crew

The crew consists of the people who are responsible for setting the stage and shifting scenery during performances.

In large houses, union stage hands are the crew. In small houses, the crew may consist of anyone from the star to the ushers. The following rules apply in either case. Each member of the crew must:

1 Accept the unadulterated fact that the stage manager rules supreme.

    A—Make sure he knows what his own responsibilities are during set-up and scene shifts.

    B—Report on time for setting the stage.

    C—Have first scene completely set by half hour.

    D—Check to see that every item he is responsible for changing is in its proper place and ready for changing.

    E—Move exactly what he has been told to move and nothing else.

    F—Place it exactly where he has been told to place it and no place else.

    G—Move it at the exact time he has been told to move it and at no other time.

    H—Move quickly and quietly at all times.

    I—Move out of the way as soon as his assignment has been completed.

Handbook for Theatrical Apprentices

> J—Report any emergency to stage manager—immediately if next shift may be affected, after the show or at intermission if it can wait.

2 Remember that the *only* way a stage manager can tell whether he has organized the shifts correctly is to try them.
> A—Be on time for crew rehearsals, sometimes called shift rehearsals. They are as important to the final production as cast rehearsals.
>
> B—"Help" no other member of the crew during any rehearsal—except in cases of dire necessity such as broken legs or set pieces.
>
> C—Report this necessary help to stage manager immediately.
>
> D—Let the stage manager know immediately if he cannot handle his own assignment.

3 Never leave the theatre until assignment is completed, i.e., stage cleared and/or furniture covered, etc.

CHAPTER 12

The Director

The director is the person responsible for transforming the author's written words into a live production.

In other words, the director must co-ordinate the four basic ingredients of any production—the choice of the play, the physical production, the cast, and the action or interpretation of the play. Each will be discussed separately.

CHOICE OF THE PLAY. The director must:

1 Select the play or agree to the producer's selection. He must consider:

   A—The area in which the play is to be produced.

   B—The physical plant in which the play will be produced.

   C—The number and kind of sets, costumes, lighting effects, etc., the budget will allow.

   D—The number of actors the budget will allow.

   E—The star available for the play (in star companies).

   F—The other plays on the schedule.

   G—The box office value of the play's title.

   H—Whether or not he is capable of handling the play.

   I—The artistic value of the play. Alas and alack, this last can only be given strong con-

sideration *if* the theatre is already an established financial success or privately endowed.
2 After the play is selected he must study it thoroughly in order to carry on with the other aspects of production.

THE PHYSICAL PRODUCTION

The director must schedule conferences with his technical staff so that he can:

1 Approve the set.
    A—Decide with the scene designer on the style of the settings, taking both practicality and final effectiveness into consideration.
    B—Demand and check floor plans and color sketches far enough in advance to give scene designer time for making necessary and/or desirable changes before construction begins.
    C—Check furniture prop list with scene designer before it is turned over to prop man.
    D—Insist that all workable parts of the set be ready for tech rehearsal.
    E—Make it absolutely clear that a *complete* set is expected for dress rehearsal.

2 Approve the props. (May be done through stage-manager.)
    A—Give basic prop list to prop man on first day of rehearsal.
    B—State what kind of prop is needed. For example: If a frying pan is on the prop list, whether it should be an old-fashioned iron skillet, a bright aluminum pan, or glass pan.
    C—State definitely when he wants actual props to be used.
    D—State definitely when he wants a reasonable

facsimile of props, i.e., something in the actors' hands.

3 Approve the sound effects.

 A—Explain to sound technician what kind of records and other sound effects he wants.

 B—State when he wants to listen to sound.

 C—Listen to the music and choose the section of the record he wants used.

 D—See that records are marked with chalk or tape (actually this is responsibility of sound technician).

 E—Set readings for music.

 F—Set cues for music coming in or out.

 G—State whether music should come in suddenly or fade up slowly, etc.

 H—Co-ordinate music and other sound effects with action no later than tech rehearsal. (Sooner will be appreciated by actors, especially if music is to back long portions of dialogue or pantomime.)

4 Approve the costumes.

 A—Check the costume plot with the costumier to see that they both have similar ideas on costuming the play—by the first rehearsal.

 B—Tell the costumier when and if any actor has special business involving a costume—as soon as he knows it. For example: If the husband has special business of zipping up his wife's dress in the bedroom scene, it is most helpful for the costumier to know this before he carefully prepares a costume that buttons up the front.

5 Approve the lighting.

 A—Go over basic lighting plan with lighting designer early in the rehearsal week to see that

Handbook for Theatrical Apprentices 57

they have similar ideas on lighting the show. (Third day should be soon enough unless special equipment is needed for the particular show.)

B—Give light cues to stage manager as they come up in rehearsal.

C—Whenever possible set the readings, colors, etc., with light man before tech rehearsal. In stock this frequently must wait until after an afternoon tech rehearsal because of light leaks in many summer theatres.

D—Set light cues during tech rehearsal.

E—Be ready, willing and able to conduct a light rehearsal after dress rehearsal if the lighting has not worked properly. Unfortunately, the time lapse between striking an old set, putting a new one up, and dress rehearsal makes this a necessity, especially if there are light leaks in the theatre. The director need not be a lighting expert, but he must know what he wants, and be able to ask for it in understandable terms. If this is so, he has a right to expect lighting to be nearly right for dress rehearsal.

6 Let the stage manager in on *everything*. (See Chapter 28—The Stage Manager.)

7 Take notes on all aspects of the physical production at tech and dress rehearsals, and give them to each department head.

NOTE: The director must make it clear to each department head that he expects to be able to do this *at dress rehearsal and not opening night!*

A—The director, scene designer, costumier, prop man, and lighting designer need at least one chance to see whether small changes would improve the final production. For example: If the book case isn't painted by dress rehearsal, it is impossible to tell whether blue or yellow flowers would look better on the coffee table. If all the men don't wear their suits under reasonably correct lighting, it is impossible to tell whether they will look too much alike or not, etc., etc.

B—If big jobs are left until the last minute, there will be no time to add the little touches that make the difference between an adequate physical production and an excellent one—even if director and staff agree that they are needed.

C—Actors need at least one chance to "get the feeling" of the set, props, sound effects, costumes and lighting, and the pace of the show withal.

THE CAST

Casting a resident company is probably the most difficult job any director will ever have to face, but he must:

1 Decide upon a cast. He must try to make sure that each person in the resident company has:

A—Audience appeal. Defining this quality is as impossible as getting along without it. It turns up in all shapes and sizes. Every performer in any phase of show business needs it in one form or another. A good director knows how to spot it, but so far as I know, there are no special rules to guide him. He must rely on his own experience and intuition.

B—Ability to get along with others. People must work together for long hours. Sometimes in stock they must eat, live, and play together. When many vital people work in such close contact, personality clashes are bound to occur occasionally. Careful casting can keep them to a minimum. Bad tempers, petulance, and childish bickering are contagious. They grow and multiply like mosquitoes. They can not be written off as mere examples of artistic temperament. They are pests. Pests detract from the efficiency of other sensitive members of the company. Fortunately (and contrary to popular opinion), they are seldom accompanied by real acting ability. Even if they are, they are hardly worth it. Avoid them at all costs.

C—Self-discipline. An actor must know his own capabilities. He must be willing to put aside his personal pleasures and problems to concentrate the time and energy necessary (for him) to work at top capacity.

D—Versatility. A resident company—whether composed of summer stock actors or community theatre members—is almost the only frontier left where versatility is an essential asset. In one show an actor may play a fussbudget French father, in the next a stalwart Irish lover, and next, a clean-cut American egghead—and so on throughout the season. He will play drama, comedy, and farce. He will perform in classics and junk. He will play bits and leads. Even the most accomplished actor will be more effective in some parts than others, but he must be able to adapt his physical characteristics and his techniques to many roles without seeming ludicrous.

E—Experience. There is no substitute. Beauty, talent, clever direction, able supporting casts, personality, vitality, diligence or youth (ah, especially youth) may cover for it—often does, as a matter of fact; but never for a whole cast, and never, never, never for a whole season. Inexperience simply requires more time and attention than there is to give.

F—Knowledge of theatre policy. The director should explain as much and as truthfully as he can about the area, theatre plant, living conditions, rehearsal schedules, etc., before signing a professional actor. He may lose an actor who seems desirable, but the odds are that he will avoid much unpleasantness later.

G—Honesty. No human being, including directors, is infallible. Acting jobs being at such a premium, actors do put their best foot forward at interviews. They do say they have backgrounds which they do not have, or that they were excellent in parts in which they were barely adequate. The wisest policy is to check with several other people with whom the actor has worked. If the director checks with only one unknown person, he may discover too late that that person is a pest (see Section B) and he has lost a very fine actor because of it.

H—Wardrobe. I apologize for bringing this one up. It seems so mercenary, but the fact remains. An actor who owns a reasonably decent wardrobe will save endless hours for himself and the costumier—on errands, alterations, and fittings, not to mention the money saved for renting, special purchases, etc. *And* audiences just do like to see well-dressed people on the stage. I may add, however (and it is not just to soothe my conscience), that an excellent wardobe cannot replace any one of the other seven requirements. It is just nice if it can accompany them.

2 After the director has assembled this appealing, pleasant, disciplined, versatile, experienced, well-informed, honest, and well-dressed company, he has the privilege of starting all over again with each production. He must give each show the advantage of the best possible casting—within the limits of his company. At the same time he cannot run the risk of exhausting one performer from playing too many leads while another is left to skylarking and griping about the fact that he hasn't had a chance to act all season.

ACTION OR INTERPRETATION

There is an argument extant that if the play is good, the physical production, beautiful, and the cast well-chosen, the director is a useless and unnecessary appendage. Not quite. No actor can see his own work, or indeed the work of other players while he is busy playing his own role; therefore, he cannot possibly judge his own work in relationship to that of the other players. True, each actor will, or should, have his own interpretation of the play. Each interpretation may be a valid one. Each actor may "feel" his own movements. These movements may also be valid, for his character. Without a director to integrate these actions and interpretations, rehearsals could turn into a bedlam of discussions (not to mention fights). The performance, no matter how brilliant, could turn the final production into hodge-podge. For an exaggerated example: A sensitive and subtle character actor "feels" that the best way to show that he finally understands his older son is to reach out silently and put his hand on his son's head. He may "feel" that upstage center is the best place for this action to take place. Meanwhile downstage center left, an exuberant and appealing juvenile "feels" that he can best show his indifference by turning back flips while eating a banana. Obviously a director is essential to the unity of the final production, whether he serves as a dictator, guide, or selector. He must:

1. Continue to study the play in relationship to his cast and physical production.
2. Make the necessary cuts in the play—before the first rehearsal if at all feasible. Of course, additional cuts may be necessary because of set or cast problems.
3. Suggest rewrites to the author if it is a new play.
4. Post (or have the stage manager post) the cast list for each new show before the first rehearsal.
5. Post (or have the stage manager post) a rehearsal schedule.
6. Give out sides or playbooks at the first rehearsal. (Sooner, if they are available and he is sure of his casting.)
7. Explain the set to his entire cast and show them a floor plan or drawing of the set.
8. Explain briefly his method of working. Directors work in many different ways. Some prefer to have the actors read through the entire play first; then discuss the various aspects of the script—plot, characters, theatrical effects, etc.; then put the

actors on the stage to more or less feel their way about, making necessary changes and adjustments as they go along. Others start by basically blocking the show, i.e., enter center, cross down right area, cross down center area, cross up left area, etc.; then work out motivations, bits of business, and interpretation later.

Still others block rather meticulously from the beginning—working out the basic blocking, small business, characterization, interpretation, motivation and timing, scene by scene, or more precisely, segment by segment.

These thumb-nail descriptions are over simplified, of course. Most directors use some personally devised combination of the three, and interchange them to suit the play, the players, and the rehearsal period.

Any method can work provided the director can communicate his ideas to each member of the cast, using each actor's creative ability as well as his own. Somehow he must impart to the actor faith in himself, confidence in his director, understanding of his role, and just plain old-fashioned enthusiasm.

9 Block the action. (Unfortunately many so-called directors believe their job begins and ends here.)
10 Not waste rehearsal time.
    A—Be on time for rehearsals.
    B—Insist on punctuality from his cast and crew.
    C—Not "freeze" his actors by being too overbearing, particularly at early rehearsals.
    D—Neither instigate nor allow an *overabundance* of unrelated banter to dissipate rehearsal time.

E—Discourage (in fact, forbid) childish bickering on the set.

11 Let the stage manager in on *everything*. (See Chapter 28 on The Stage Manager.)
12 Set the curtain calls.
13 Take notes during final run-throughs, tech and dress rehearsals.
14 Give constructive notes to cast and technical staff following final run-throughs and rehearsals. (May be given during intermissions if director prefers.)
15 Give best wishes to cast and crew at half hour on opening night. (Not necessary, but nice.)
16 Turn the entire production over to the stage manager at half hour on opening night.

   A—For better or worse, the stage manager must have complete authority back stage during performance. Naturally, if some drastic thing happens which the stage manager cannot possibly see, but which can be corrected, the director should let him know about it. For example: If an actor becomes so carried away with his own inner feelings that he cannot be heard (this happens all too frequently with inexperienced players) the director may *ask the stage manager* to tell him to speak up.

   B—During performance each actor's part must belong to him alone. After the final curtain call, the director's notes, criticisms, and suggestions are not only appreciated but sought by serious actors. During the show he is, or should be, the forgotten man. He is about as useful back stage as "mother" is in a bridal suite.

FOOTNOTE FOR COMMUNITY THEATRES ONLY: In most

community theatres the director must assume most of the tasks designated for The Producer. (See Chapter 21.) I therefore have one additional bit of advice which I believe to be of utmost importance to all NEW Community Theatre groups. HIRE A DIRECTOR! The larger and long-established community theatres have a paid director, scene designer and technical director, business manager, publicity director, secretary, etc. The theatre group will be able to tell what other paid personnel it needs as it grows and becomes more successful. But right from the very beginning there must be someone *in charge* who has the training, temperament, and time to organize and utilize the local talent.

Believe me, there are many gifted actors, painters, carpenters, electricians, pianists, singers, dancers, etc., in many communities. All these talents want, and should have, a chance for expression in the community theatre. Unfortunately chaos, quarrels, cliques, tears, and diminishing interest always result unless some *one* is in charge. He cannot do all the work. He will need the co-operation of every member of the community theatre and the support of a strong board of directors.

The first director a community theatre hires may not be the right one for that particular community, but that does not invalidate the original premise. I repeat: HIRE A DIRECTOR, and give him complete co-operation and authority for as long as he is director.

CHAPTER 13

The Dresser

The dresser is the person responsible for seeing that a particular performer arrives on stage in the proper costume for each entrance. He must:

1. Find out what the performer wears for his first entrance.
2. Find out from the performer what is to be removed and what is to be added for each succeeding entrance.
3. Find out what the exit line is before each costume change.
4. Determine the amount of time available for costume change.
5. Decide with the performer where is the best place to make each costume change; i.e., off stage right, off stage left, in the performer's dressing room, and so forth.
6. Determine with the performer what part of each change the performer will do and what he wants the dresser to do.
7. Check *all* items for each costume change before the first curtain.
8. Have safety pins handy in case of emergency.
9. Be at the designated place with all items for the costume change at the correct time. (Even seconds too late can ruin an entrance!)
10. Make changes quickly, quietly, and with a min-

imum of movement (particularly during quick changes in close quarters).

11 Take discarded costumes back to performer's dressing room and hang them up after each change.
12 Check all costumes before leaving the theatre after each performance. Report any necessary repairs, cleaning, pressing, etc., to wardrobe mistress.
13 Never appear nervous or harassed, even during extremely fast changes.

CHAPTER **14**

The Electrician

The electrician is the person responsible for the execution of all lighting connected with a production.

In almost all resident companies the job of electrician is combined with that of lighting designer (see Chapter 16), though each job is quite distinct. To make it clear for those companies who do have two men for the job, or who combine scenery and lighting design, director and lighting designer, etc., the two phases of lighting a show will be discussed separately here—with the plea that all lighting designers and electricians find out before they accept either position whether or not they are to handle both.

The electrician must:

1 Accept complete responsibility for the preparation and care of electrical equipment.

At the beginning of the season:

    A—Determine what usable equipment he has on hand.

    B—Check safety of every piece of his equipment.

    C—Store articles which need repair in a separate place marked "DANGEROUS, DO NOT USE."

    D—Make necessary repairs, starting with equipment needed in the first show, and continuing steadily until all equipment is in working order.

E—Get rid of material which can not be repaired. (NOTE: Expensive items should be reported to management for obsolescence tax purposes.)

F—Find out what sources are available for obtaining additional lighting equipment in the area.

G—Determine what new equipment is necessary.

H—Determine what new equipment is desirable. (NOTE: Remember the budget.)

I—Have business manager or producer verify orders for new equipment.

J—Order new equipment immediately upon verification.

(1) Not wait until air express delivery is necessary, thus squandering the budget.

(2) Not wait until fear that the lights won't arrive on time causes useless tension.

K—Keep records of all purchases and costs.

L—Turn expense account over to business manager before opening.

M—Hang basic lighting equipment in a permanent position. Naturally some shows will require special and/or additional units which cannot be included in the above rule. The electrician will do well to remember, however, that the less precious time, energy, and plain muscular strength he must use for the basics in each production, the more he has for obtaining certain special or showy effects.

N—Use utmost precaution in hanging all units. Each item must be absolutely secure.

O—Keep floor wires out of actors' and crew's way as much as possible.

P—Remember that a switchboard is a delicate machine.
 (1) Treat it gently.
 (2) Keep it cleaned and oiled.
 (3) Make sure that dimmers are "up full" when not in use.

Q—Keep several flashlights within reach at all times.

R—Find out the capacity of the switchboard and never exceed its limit.

S—Find out the capacity of each fuse (or breaker) and never exceed the maximum limit.

T—Find out the capacity of *each* dimmer and never exceed its limit.

U—Make it absolutely clear that novices are not to handle electrical equipment without proper supervision.

V—Know when the help and/or advice of an expert licensed electrician is needed for specialized jobs such as installing new wiring and equipment, or checking safety.

W—Know whom to call for such emergencies.

X—Be responsible for getting expert help when it is needed.

Y—See that dressing rooms and work rooms, i.e., prop room, costume room, paint room offices, etc., are equipped with lights of proper intensity and placement.

Z—See that the stage work light is in working

order and that the switch is easily accessible to the stage manager.

NOTE: It is pleasant if the work light is bright enough to permit actors to read their sides during rehearsals.

For each production:

A—Continue to follow above rules concerning safety and expenses.

B—Return borrowed or rented materials in good condition within three days after its final use. (Sooner if feasible.)

C—Keep unused equipment in clean, dry place.

At the end of the season:

A—Take inventory of all equipment.

B—Give inventory list to management.

C—Report worn-out or unsafe equipment to management.

D—Repair defective equipment (if time allows).

E—Store unrepaired equipment in a separate place. Mark it "DANGEROUS, DO NOT USE."

F—Label all equipment and/or boxes in which it is stored.

G—Store all equipment in a clean dry place.

H—Return all borrowed or rented equipment in good condition.

I—Give final record of purchases and costs to business manager.

2 Operate the switchboard during performances.

A—Make (or obtain from lighting designer) a complete light plot including every light unit to be used in the show, its position and direction. (Not later than three days before tech rehearsal.)

B—Obtain necessary additional equipment, including gelatins, and have it ready for use.

(Not later than one day before technical rehearsal and sooner if within the realm of possibility.)

C—Make (or obtain from light designer) a tentative cue sheet including every light change from the dimming of the house lights through their coming up again after final curtain call. The cue sheet should include:

(1) Set-up of lights at the beginning of each act.

(2) Warn cues for light changes.

(3) Cues for light changes.

(4) Light changes—switch numbers, outlet numbers, dimmer numbers, and intensities should be marked plainly on each set-up and change.

D—Focus the lights according to light plot before the first technical rehearsal.

E—Have a light rehearsal according to cue sheet, in collaboration with director and designer.

NOTE: In stock, if the strike and setting up of the new set have been organized correctly, light rehearsal can take place before dawn breaks on strike night.

If the electrician sees that a reasonable rehearsal cannot be held at this time, he should go home as soon as he finishes setting up his lights. He will need his strength and his wits about him for a grueling tech rehearsal, dress rehearsal, and lighting rehearsal which will undoubtedly follow dress rehearsal. (Pity.) During the lighting rehearsal he must:

(1) Have someone walk the sets to make sure there are no undesirable dead spots or hot spots.

(2) Readjust lights and set intensities.

(3) Write necessary corrections on the cue sheet as he sees them or according to director's notes. The memory simply cannot be trusted.

F—Run lights according to cue sheet during tech rehearsal. Make necessary corrections in lighting and cue sheet during tech rehearsal (or immediately following tech rehearsal if there is no time to make corrections during the rehearsal).

G—Run lights according to corrected cue sheet during dress rehearsal.

H—Become familiar with cue sheet and its relationship to the entire production.

I—Take a quick check of lights before half hour at each performance. Many a scene has been ruined because, according to the electrician, "Someone unplugged the moonlight," or "Someone knocked the down left spot out of focus."

J—Run lights with care and accuracy during *every* performance.

K—Turn outside lights, theatre lights, and house lights on at designated time before each performance.

L—Kill all lights before leaving theatre after each performance.

NOTE: If for any reason certain lights are to be left on for a long period following any performance, the electrician must turn this responsibility over to a reliable individual.

3 See CHAPTER 16 on LIGHT DESIGNER—if job is coupled with that of designing lights.

CHAPTER 15

The Jobber

Jobbers are actors who come into a company to play one or more parts, but who are not members of the resident acting company, the staff, or the apprentice group. Jobbers are divided into two categories—professional and local.

1 A professional jobber in stock is usually hired to:
   A—Play a part which does not suit the capabilities of anyone in the resident company.
   B—Make up the Equity quota of union members needed in large-cast shows.
   C—Release a resident actor from the grind of playing leads every single week.
   D—Promote interest by adding freshness and variety to the usual cast.
   E—Give the publicity director a new subject to exploit. A jobber should always arrive on the scene with numerous photographs, a supply of "who's who" material and all the charm he can muster.
   F—Publicize the theatre (and incidentally himself) by using his "free" time to give T.V., radio, and newspaper interviews; to judge beauty contests, baby contests, or art shows (about which he may know nothing, but no matter); to appear at luncheons, cocktail parties, club meetings, swimming meets, tid-

dledewink games, or any place else that may be frequented by potential ticket buyers.
2 The professional jobber is *not* hired to:
   A—Bask in the sun.
   B—Demand apprentices to polish his sun glasses or perform other servile tasks.
   C—Point out the advantages of other companies.
   D—Lecture on the crass stupidity of being a resident actor.
   E—Pile up debts or romantic conquests all over town. (This tends to place a stigma on all theatrical personnel).
3 The professional jobber must also remember that he is *part of the cast* and follow the rules accordingly. (See CHAPTER 6—THE CAST.)
Local jobbers are usually people who are interested in the theatre, but who have little time to devote to it. Ordinarily, they perform without pay.
4 A local jobber is usually engaged to:
   A—Play a part which does not suit the physical type of any member of the resident company, including staff, or apprentices.
   B—Release a company actor for a larger or more demanding role.
   C—Save the salary and transportation costs necessary for hiring a professional jobber.
   At first glance it may seem that by doing the management a favor (which he is!) the local jobber is furthering the unemployment rate among professional actors. *Not so*. Without the local jobber many theatres would not be able to meet production costs and would have to close. Obviously this

would drive even more professional actors into the ranks of the unemployed.

D—Promote interest by adding freshness and variety to the usual cast.

(1) New audiences will come to see their friends perform.

(2) These new audiences may become regular customers.

E—Inspire additional publicity. Local newspapers are almost always willing to print personal items about residents of the area. Local jobbers should never be hesitant about furnishing pictures, stories, or suggestions of newspaper, radio, or T.V. personnel in the area who may be interested in special news items or stories about them.

F—Stimulate a friendly relationship between local residents and the theatre company.

Some professional theatre people are wont to believe that the word "local" is always followed by the word "yokel." Residents of some areas believe that the word "actor" should always be prefaced by "crazy," "stuck-up," or "crack-pot." Both theories can usually be dispelled if the two groups are brought together.

5 Local jobbers should remember that they are part of the cast and do their best to follow the rules for the cast. (See CHAPTER 6, THE CAST.)

NOTE: It is understood that local jobbers may not be able to attend full-time rehearsals, the fittings as scheduled, etc. They should, however, make arrangements for special rehearsals, fittings, pictures, etc., before agreeing to be in a show. Most of them do this as a matter of course because: (1) They really love the theatre or they wouldn't give their time and energy to it. (2) They do not wish to make fools of themselves before their friends. Indeed, the high quality performances of some local jobbers puts them in the "Pro" (if not professional) category.

CHAPTER 16

The Lighting Designer

The lighting designer is the person who is responsible for planning the lights for a production. He must:

1. Draw a light plot (sometimes called light layout) showing the setting and position of all the light units to be used in a production. In order to do this he should:

    A—Be aware of all practical phases of the electrician's job.

NOTE: In almost all resident companies the jobs of electrician and lighting designer are combined. (See CHAPTER 14.)

   B—Study the play and plan lighting effects to enhance the play, not overshadow it.

   C—Confer with the director and the scene designer to make sure that all three are working toward the same effect.

   D—Bear in mind that the audience would like to see the actors' faces.

   E—Know what equipment the theatre owns.

   F—Use that equipment to obtain desired effects whenever possible.

   G—Know what equipment is available at near-by sources.

   H—Use that equipment to augment theatre equipment when necessary.

    I—Keep light plans simple enough to be mounted properly in the time allowed.
NOTE: Whenever possible, leave basic units in their permanent position.
    J—Not demand effects which will cause overloading.
  2 Complete his basic plans by the third day of rehearsal so he can:
    A—Check with the electrician on the practicality of his plans.
    B—Give electrician time to obtain and/or prepare all necessary equipment in advance.
    C—Make necessary changes.
  3 Make a tentative cue sheet which will include:
    A—Set-up of lights at the beginning of each act.
    B—Light changes.
    C—Warn cues for light changes.
    D—Cues for light changes.
NOTE: Switch numbers, outlet numbers, and dimmer numbers should be marked on each set-up and change.
    E—Check with stage manager to see that someone is available to make backstage changes, such as changing gelatins, plugging, unplugging, etc.
    F—Not procrastinate on any of the above if he is also the electrician.
  4 Check lighting effects with electrician and scene designer and director (if available) as soon as both sets and lights are up. In stock this would be, hopefully, before dawn on strike night.
  5 Check lighting effects during tech and dress rehearsals.
  6 Give electrician notes for necessary corrections.
  7 Be prepared to have a final light rehearsal following dress rehearsal if necessary.

CHAPTER 17

The Maintenance Man

The maintenance man is the person responsible for keeping the theatre and its grounds in tip-top condition throughout the season. He must:

1. Realize that the condition of the theatre and its grounds on opening night is as important to the success of the season as the first production on stage. The bulk of the work must be done pre-season.
2. Accept responsibility for care of his own equipment.
    A—Check supplies at the beginning of the season.
    B—List additional equipment necessary, including approximate cost.
    C—Have above list approved by business manager.
    D—Order supplies immediately.
    E—Keep accounts of all pre-season expenses.
    F—Turn above accounts over to business manager *before* opening.
    G—Find out in advance where power equipment, such as lawn mowers, sweepers, etc., can be repaired quickly and inexpensively. Never wait for an emergency.
    H—Find out in advance who is a reliable

plumber, where he can be reached, and if he will come for an emergency.

I—Designate specific storage place for each item when not in use:
  (1) Racks for brooms.
  (2) Hooks for dust pans.
  (3) Rack for hose.
  (4) Hooks for watering cans.
  (5) Shelves for cleaning supplies, such as cleansers, soaps, sponges, etc.
  (6) Racks for rakes, hoes, post hole diggers, etc.
  (7) Special shelves for outdoor or house paint not to be confused with scene paints.
  (8) Dry place for storing paper towels, toilet tissues, etc.
  (9) Space for lawn mower.
  (10) Space for vacuum.

J—*Insist* that assistants put items away when they stop working on a task. (That they planned to come back and finish it in two hours is no excuse.)

K—Check supplies weekly and reorder necessary items personally.
  (1) Keep expense accounts.
  (2) Turn weekly accounts over to business manager. Nothing is more annoying to a business manager than to have a dozen apprentices show up with 10-, 25-, and 50-cent expense accounts for purchasing two rolls of toilet paper, a box of soap flakes, a box of tacks, etc.

3 See that grounds are kept.

A—Mow the lawn as many times as necessary to keep it smooth and green.

  B—Clip areas which cannot be reached with lawn mower.
  C—Replant grass in bare areas.
  D—Trim hedges.
  E—Plant flowers in designated areas.
  F—Weed flowers weekly.
  G—Water flowers daily (in a dry season, of course).
  H—Place garbage cans in strategic places.
  I—Place butt cans filled with sand in strategic places.
  J—Remove junk, including cigarette butts, daily.
  K—Rake when necessary.
4 Check daily to see that out-door furniture (if any) is kept in good repair:
  A—Safe. (No broken chair legs, tippy benches, protruding nails, etc.)
  B—Clean. (Usually needs to be wiped off daily an hour or so before curtain.)
  C—Freshly painted. (Usually once at the beginning of the season is sufficient.) Need I add that "WET PAINT" signs must be prominent until paint is absolutely dry?
5 See that all stairways, indoors and out, are kept in good repair.
6 Make sure that all seats are in safe condition for every performance.
  A—Ask ushers to report broken or loose seats.
  B—Ask ushers to report missing numbers on seats.
  C—If slip-covers or head rests are used, see that they are kept clean and neatly attached.
  D—Vacuum or dust seats daily.

NOTE: Chemically treated dust cloths are a boon to dusters.

7 Hang house decorations securely.

NOTE: These will differ according to the motif of the theatre. For example: barn theatres may use old wagon wheels, ploughs, gourds, etc.; a tent theatre may use old circus posters, banners, etc.; a really plush theatre may use sconces, paintings, etc. *But* whatever the motif, the decorations must be kept clean, neat, and safe.

8 Hang house, lounge, and lobby curtains if used.
    A—See that they are put up securely.
    B—See that they are kept clean.
    C—Ask ushers to straighten them before doors open nightly.

9 Clean house daily.
    A—*Leave nothing in the aisles*.
    B—Vacuum or sweep floor.

NOTE: Sprinkling before sweeping will lighten dust problems.

    C—Dust railings.
    D—Clean stairways.

10 Keep rest rooms attractive and *sanitary*. See that they are:
    A—Freshly painted or papered when necessary. (Usually once at the beginning of the season is sufficient.)
    B—In perfect working order.
        (1) Have plunger handy.
        (2) Call plumber immediately if he cannot handle disorder.
    C—Scrubbed and disinfected daily.
    D—Supplied with toilet tissue, soap, paper towels and cups, daily.
    E—Waste cans are emptied daily.

11 Clean lounge and/or lobby daily.

A—Vacuum.
B—Dust.
C—Clean ashtrays.
D—Empty waste baskets.
E—Replace wilted flowers.
F—Water potted plants.
G—Put publicity literature in selected spots.

12 Assign specific weekly tasks to assistants. Naturally no one man could possibly achieve all the little duties necessary for maintaining a theatre. In order to use his assistants wisely he must:

A—Post definite tasks for assistants, i.e., one to house, one to rest rooms, one to lounge, etc.
B—Divide tasks fairly, keeping in mind that no blossoming young thespian wants to clean rest rooms *every* week.
C—Make sure that every assistant knows every chore connected with his assignment and the deadline for its achievement.
D—Keep and post a list of odd chores to be accomplished so that everyone who has a free moment can be useful.
E—Never hesitate to assign chores from the above list to local jobbers, apprentices, ushers, or just plain well-wishers who are willing to do something to help the theatre.
   (1) Have equipment ready.
   (2) Explain chore simply.
   (3) Show gratitude.

13 Clean windows regularly.

14 See that equipment is cleaned, stored, and inventoried at the end of the season.

A—Turn inventory over to management at the end of the season.
B—See that grounds are left clean.

Handbook for Theatrical Apprentices 85

    C—Make arrangements for turning off water and draining pipes in areas where freezing could occur.
    D—See that all drapes, seatcovers, etc. are left clean and moth balled.
    E—See that rat poison is left in strategic places. (Particularly necessary in barn theatres.)
    F—See that house is left clean, as safe as possible, and securely locked.
15 Turn keys over to management upon leaving.

CHAPTER 18

Musical Director

The musical director is the person responsible for the execution of instrumental music used in the show.

Musicals in summer stock may be performed with any combination of musical instruments from one piano to a full orchestra. The musical director must:

1. Have a fair knowledge of the music to be used.
2. Be ready, willing, and able to change keys and/or tempo to suit a particular production.
3. Co-operate with book director, choreographer, and choral director in setting up rehearsal schedules for principals and chorus.
4. Stick to rehearsal schedules.
5. Set keys for performers at earliest possible moment.
6. Try to be calm and helpful when actors who cannot sing are assigned musical roles.

NOTE: It won't help to hide under the piano or climb on top of it and scream when an actor says, "Oh, just play it any way you want to. I don't go by key anyway."

7. Mark changes in music as they are determined in rehearsal.
8. Mark warn cues and music cues *lightly* in his score during rehearsals.
9. Mark warn cues and music cues *plainly* when they are definitely set by director, choreographer, musical director, and performers. (See 13.)

10 Not change tempo mid-performance.
   A—Accept the inevitable fact that some of the following remarks will be made occasionally.
   B—Take heed, i.e., look for other work, when the following remarks are made with great frequency.

REMARKS: "No one in his right mind could kick *that* fast." "He never played it *that* fast before." "What's he? Got a date after the show? Wants to get it over with quick?" "Gee, we coulda' killed ourselves," etc., etc., etc. Or "Whatzit? A funeral dirge we got?" "I know this bird don't care, but I was *up* there!" "He lays an egg, and I have it all over my face." "I coulda' read a book between those turns." "He never played it like *that* in rehearsals." "If he'd only just pick it up, pick it up, pick it up." "That ruined my applause exit." Etc., etc., etc.

11 Be on time for performances.
12 Be dressed properly for performances.

NOTE: Rules for wardrobe are about the same as they are for members of the cast. Musicians are responsible for their own modern clothes, but if they are to be costumed (i.e., blazers and straw hats for 20's shows, cowboy suits for westerns, etc.) they should arrange for fittings during early part of their rehearsal schedule. Mad and mussed-up musicians are fine in rehearsal, but in performance, their "get-ups" should not attract unnecessary attention or comment.

13 Erase all markings on score and return it to the stage manager not later than one day after the final performance.
14 If an orchestra is used, the musical director must also:
   A—Come to terms on budget with the producer before musicians are hired.
   B—Choose musicians.

C—See that each member of the orchestra has a score.
D—Call music rehearsals.
E—Give changes as determined in rehearsal to each musician.
F—Collect music after last performance.
G—Check to see that all markings have been erased.
H—Return all scores to the stage manager.

CHAPTER 19

The Patron's Chairman

The patron's chairman is the person responsible for selling "season" or subscription tickets. He must:

1 Determine what kind of subscription tickets will sell best in his area. There are several kinds:

    A—A book of tickets, sold at a reduced rate, which may be used in any combination that the buyer wishes, i.e., he may buy one book of ten tickets and use it to see ten shows, or he may bring a party of ten and use all the tickets for one performance. The buyer must, in this instance, call the box office to make reservations each time he wishes to use his ticket.

    B—A punch ticket which allows the buyer to see each show on any night that he chooses. These tickets are usually sold at a reduced rate, and the buyer must call the box office to make reservations for the night he chooses to attend.

    C—A season ticket which entitles the buyer to his own seat, on his own night for each show during the season. These tickets may or may not be sold at a reduced rate, but they do save the buyer the inconvenience of making reservations each week, deciding which night

90   Handbook for Theatrical Apprentices

to go—and making special arrangements each week for baby-sitters, etc.

2 Find himself several assistants to represent him in different sections of the city and/or in each small town in the area.

    A—See that every assistant has all the necessary information for selling tickets.

    B—Determine and let each assistant know what remuneration or benefits he will receive.

    C—Impress upon assistants that they are *not* asking for help from potential buyers, but offering a service.

3 Make pre-season preparations for subscription drive well in advance.

    A—Make a list (with the help of assistants) of all the people he wishes to reach:

        (1) Those who have been subscribers before.

        (2) Those who have come to the theatre often.

        (3) Those who come to the theatre occasionally.

        (4) Those who are active in other community projects, but have not added theatre to their list.

        (5) Newcomers to the area.

        (6) Friends of the above.

    B—Determine the date to start the subscription drive.

    C—Compose an initial letter containing:

        (1) Information about the theatre.

        (2) Information about the dates of performance.

        (3) Information about the prices (for season and other).

(4) Information about the shows to be presented (if the schedule is not complete, information about the kind of shows may be substituted, i.e., recent Broadway hits, classic, musical, drama, reviews, etc.).

(5) A phone number for calling in orders and a time when office will be open.

(6) A form for ordering tickets by mail.

(7) A space for saying a check is enclosed or send bill on the first of the month.

(8) A request for suggestions of other persons who may be interested in subscription tickets.

(9) Last date for ordering subscription tickets.

D—Write newspaper releases containing above information.

E—Compose another letter thanking buyer for his patronage and stating that tickets are enclosed.

F—Design tickets. (This of course, may be left to printer, if he is given all the necessary information.)

G—Order the above letters, tickets, envelopes, self-addressed envelopes, order blanks from printers. Specify date that each must be ready. (Allow time for delay!)

H—Either design ads to announce season ticket drive—or get ads from publicity director.

4 Start the drive on determined date.

A—Send or take ads to the papers in plenty of time to have them properly placed on date determined for starting the subscription drive.

B—If possible get releases on the drive into

papers about the same time as ad will appear. (Usually the chairman and his assistants will know someone personally who can get this information into the newspapers, local radio programs, local T.V. programs.)

C—Address letters to all potential ticket buyers, stuff them, stamp them, and *put them in the mail* no later than beginning date of subscription drive.

D—Approximately one week after ads have appeared and letters have been mailed, follow up letters with phone calls.

5 Keep accurate up-to-date accounts of patrons, tickets, and money.

  A—Keep list and mark off names of those who have bought tickets.
  B—Check whether each ticket has or has not been paid for.
  C—Be prompt in sending tickets to subscribers.
  D—Double check to make sure that each subscriber is sent the correct tickets.
  E—Deposit subscription money upon receipt and keep complete accounts of it.
  F—Give complete accounts of money spent and money received to business manager.

6 Add to—but do not substitute for—the above efficiency rules promotional ideas of his own:

  A—Which are courteous.
  B—Which are honest.
  C—Which can be followed through.
  D—Which the patron's chairman (and his assistants) have every intention of following through.
  E—Which will promote good public relations for the theatre.

CHAPTER 20

The Photographer

The photographer is the person responsible for producing pictures needed (or wanted) by the management, the publicity director, and the cast.

He is not usually a member of the theatre staff, but a local photographer who comes in one night a week after a performance and takes pictures of the set and the actors which may be bought by management or members of the company. He must:

1 Set the time that he will shoot pictures and be willing to stick to that schedule.

   A— Arrive with his camera loaded and the number of flash bulbs he will need.

   B—Find out from stage manager what shots are wanted *before* the company is called.

   (1) Set shots (to be determined by the designer).

   (2) Action shots (to be determined by the director).

   (3) Publicity shots (to be determined by the publicity director).

   (4) Pictures for the photographer's own amusement or monetary gain.

NOTE: Remember that most actors who have reached the leading-man, leading-woman, or character-actor status have a trunk full of pictures stashed away somewhere.

The pictures that will *sell* best are of juveniles, ingenues, apprentices, and local jobbers.

    C—Shoot pictures in the order that will require the least number of scenery shifts, costume changes, and people waiting, i.e., finale shots first, etc.

2 Deliver publicity pictures immediately to place designated by publicity director.

3 Deliver cast's and staff's pictures.

    A—Find out at the beginning of the season when and where he can display cast proofs for cast's ordering.

    B—Number each picture for convenience of potential buyer.

    C—Display pictures at the same time and place each week.

    D—Set deadline for ordering pictures each week.

    E—Determine the price of his pictures and ask stage manager to post price scale on the call board and wherever pictures are displayed.

    F—Set delivery date for pictures. Deliver on the same date each week. (Pay day is the perfect time.)

    G—Collect on delivery.

NOTE: Actors, by and large, are very honest people; however, they move around a lot, they have lines to learn, costumes to fit, and frequently a wolf at the door. Besides, nothing is quite so dead as last week's performance—so a wise photographer will heed this kind advice and collect on delivery.

    H—Remember that management is only responsible for the pictures ordered by the management.

CHAPTER 21

The Producer

The producer is the person who is responsible for *everything* that has anything to do with his theatre. This includes the aardvarks (first word in the dictionary) captured to rid the picnic tables of ants, the zyzzling (last word in the dictionary) of critics after a bad production, and everything in between.

NOTE: In summer stock the producer is usually one person, while in community theatre he may be the president of the group or a board of directors. For simplicity, we will in this chapter consider him or them as one person—the head man.

"Everything" may actually be divided into seven main ingredients. A producer must have:

1. A theatre, i.e., a place in which to present his plays. All sorts of places have been used as theatres:

    A—Abandoned opera houses seating thousands.
    B—Reconstructed barns seating about one hundred or more.
    C—Tents of all sizes.
    D—Hotel ball rooms.
    E—High school auditoriums.
    F—Once in a while the miracle of miracles—a theatre which was actually designed and constructed for the purpose of putting on plays.

Before the producer acquires his theatre he must make sure of one thing—that there are enough people in the area to support it. No matter how good the productions, how glamorous the theatre, how prominent the stars, or how illustrious the publicity, a theatre cannot exist without people to come to it. *After* he has found a theatre and decided that he can make it "go," he must:

> A—Set about raising the money to buy, rent, or lease the theatre. This may be done by:
> (1) Selling small shares in his company to many backers.
> (2) Finding one backer to buy or lease the theatre.

NOTE: One backer (or even two) may become co-producers, i.e., run the theatre in co-ordination with the original producer; however, if there are numerous backers the producer must see to it that he runs the show. Boards of directors may have marvelous suggestions, but one man must be responsible for final decisions. The "too many cooks" adage was never more pertinent than in the theatre.

> B—Get a good lawyer to do whatever it is that lawyers do in a situation like this. Since this is a field in itself, I will merely advise that the new producer:
> (1) Find a reputable lawyer.
> (2) Explain his situation in lay terms.
> (3) Let the lawyer handle it.
>
> C—Raise enough operation capital to keep his theatre open through at least two losing seasons.

NOTE: This, of course, is an ideal arrangement; however, if the producer is sure enough of his theatre, his area, his product, and his own ability, he must be willing to take a chance that additional backing will be forth-

Handbook for Theatrical Apprentices 97

coming after his doors are open. If it isn't, it won't kill him—or even keep him from finding another theatre in a season or two.

  2 A Policy, i.e., he must decide whether his theatre is more suited to:

    A—A star package system in stock.

        The producer provides the theatre, the production staff, the stage settings, the props, and the publicity. He books different shows which have been cast and rehearsed (and probably performed) someplace else into his theatre each week. Each show sends an advance director to the theatre about one week before production to see that the scenery is built according to plan, that the correct props are gathered, that sound, lights and other special effects will be handled in *the same way that they were handled in the last place*, and to block the bit players into *the same spots that they have been blocked* in the last place. The leading players arrive in time for dress rehearsal. The advance director sees them through and then goes on to the next theatre to see that the scenery is built according to plan, that the correct props—etc. The star package system has the same advantage as a brand name in a grocery store—customers are willing to pay more for a product they know about. The producer knows that the star's press agent has, in a way, been on his publicity staff since the first word was ever printed about said star.

        Another advantage is that the producer can expect a smooth, well-rehearsed show each week without the additional responsibility of getting it ready. He can concentrate his efforts on the physical production and the publicity.

Another advantage—the producer can avoid long association with groups he does not like.

And another advantage—the producer can meet some very interesting and exciting personalities with whom lasting friendships occasionally develop.

Still another—and important to many producers—is all the name-dropping he can do at parties for the rest of the year.

The disadvantages are that the producer and his staff must accept their places as servants to the stars. Many of the demagogues have been burned often on their way up and down the ladder. They are taking no chances on the intelligence and ability of mere strangers who happen to be running a theatre.

Another disadvantage is that while the star may bring more money into the box-office during the week, he certainly takes a large portion of it with him when he leaves on Saturday night.

Still another is the short time available for cultivating friendships with any group or individual.

The biggest disadvantage, however, stems from the advantage of not having the responsibility of getting the shows ready. The theatre producer becomes a show booker. He misses out on the creative excitement of being a play maker.

A-A—A guest star system in community theatre. The community theatre members rehearse, build their sets, etc., as for any other production; the only difference being that one or two of the leading roles are played by professional actors who are invited in for a particular production. The problem, of course, is to find the right guest star and then to get him at the time he is needed at a somewhat reasonable rate.

One advantage of having a guest star is the vast amount that local actors may learn from a *good* professional actor—not only about acting techniques but theatre lore as well.

A second advantage is the prestige it gives the theatre. Obviously the more prestige the star has, the more he will lend the theatre.

A third advantage is that an occasional star will attract new audiences who may become regular customers.

One disadvantage is that part of the income must be used to pay the professional actor.

Another disadvantage is the resentment or jealousy that may rise among local actors who are (and have been for years) donating their services.

Still another disadvantage: the professional actor may not be able to afford a full rehearsal schedule. He may expect the production to be almost ready when he arrives. (It is very difficult to learn lines and rehearse scenes with a character who is not there!)

The main disadvantage, however, is that unless the guest star has been reached through personal contact, for example, a friend of the director, or a home town boy who has made a name for himself in the professional theatre, the community theatre just might "pick a lemon."

B—A resident stock company.

The producer hires, in addition to his production staff, a group of unknown but versatile actors and a director. These actors rehearse, during the day, a new play each week. At night they perform in the play that they rehearsed last week. The advantages are:

(1) The actors are not so expensive, even though they must work harder. (One show by day—another by night.)

(2) The excitement of play making.

(3) The ensemble acting (which can occur even with a week's rehearsal) of a group which has worked together for some weeks.

(4) The pleasure of watching a fine talent develop and of helping it to develop.

(5) The co-operative spirit of a well organized resident company.

(6) The fact that the creative imagination of the staff, i.e., scene and light designer, property man, etc., can be utilized if it exists.

(7) Royalties are usually cheaper; however, they vary according to the size of the house.

(8) The producer is the boss. (He only has to answer to his backers, his audience, the press, the radio, the lumber supply company, the hardware store, Samuel French, Actor's Equity, the local ladies' clubs, etc., etc.)

The main disadvantage is that unknown actors (no matter how talented) are harder to sell, thus causing the necessity for a lower budget. Other disadvantages are:

(1) The enormous amount of work it takes to mount a new play every week.

(2) The close proximity of a diversified group of people over a relatively long period of time.

(3) The miscasting that *must* occur. (Granted that some of the most thrilling performances are the direct result of not casting to type, they are the exceptions which prove the rule—I suppose.)

(4) The necessity of having people double up on jobs for financial reasons.

For Example: The stage manager may have to play a pretty big part to save transportation and salary of an imported actor. The stage manager may be a fine actor and play his part extremely well, *but* someone else who is not nearly so qualified will have to take over at least some of his stage managing duties. Too much of this sort of thing is bound to cause noticible *gaps* in the production.

C—The non-professional company.

The non-professional company is usually

run on about the same basis as a resident company. The advantages are:

(1) The actors do not have to be paid—or perhaps they are given room and board.

(2) There are no union problems.

(3) Because of the above, the company can be larger.

(4) Royalties are usually low.

(5) Non-professional companies are usually young, hard-working and enthusiastic.

The disadvantages are:

(6) Non-professionals are even harder to sell than unknown professionals.

(7) Most young actors and technicians lack skill and technique (no matter how enthusiastic, hard working, and talented they are).

(8) The final productions are seldom as polished.

(9) In addition to his normal tasks, the producer of the very young company must serve as teacher, adviser, and mother superior.

D—The musical tent.

The musical tent may be run on the star package system or the resident company system. Most frequently it is a combination of both. The chorus and small parts are part of the resident company; they learn a new show each week. The leads (sometimes stars —sometimes not) are jobbed in for only one or two shows. They are expected to know their songs, dances and lines when they arrive. They may rehearse with the company for a week—or, as in the star package system, an advance director may come in to see that the scenery, lights, blockings, choruses, etc., fit the stars' way of playing the show. (See advance director under star package system, page 97) Musical companies frequently use non-professional local performers in small parts or to augment the chorus. The main advantages are:

(1) Almost everybody likes musicals.

(2) They have the advance publicity of record albums, radio and juke box plugs, etc., making the titles and the music known to the general public.

(3) They do not have to be as polished as a straight play to have audience appeal.

The main disadvantages:

(1) The tremendous overhead of mounting a musical—large casts, numerous sets, numerous costumes, musicians, high royalties, large production staff, maintenance of a large theatre, large parking lot, and so forth.

(2) The tremendous amount of work involved in co-ordinating all the components of a musical.

Otherwise the advantages and disadvantages are about the same as they are in other companies, in about the same ratio as each system is used to present musicals rather than straight plays.

E—The classic festival.

The classic festival may be run on any of the above mentioned plans.

More young people have probably failed with this kind of theatre than any other. Classic festivals are excellent training grounds for actors, directors, scene and costume and lighting designers. They are extremely rewarding to those who are personally involved with each production. They may have a very devoted and loyal audience —but it is frequently quite small. Audiences for a classic festival are particularly hard to find in a resort area. Costumes and settings are almost always extensive and expensive. Casts are usually large. Even competent performers are hard to find. The really experienced ones are expensive, though they can sometimes be persuaded to work for a nominal fee for the privilege of playing a favorite role.

The most likely place to succeed with a classic series is at a university theatre where the producer has access to the theatre, scenery, costumes, and student actors—not to mention student labor. If he finds himself successful, he may try a bona fide professional company. In any case he will do well to remember that most successful classic festivals are subsidized—and heavily subscribed.

3 **A budget.**

The producer must decide how funds can be most wisely spent for the purpose of maintaining and improving his theatre, presenting acceptable productions, and making a profit.

A—The budget will be affected by:

(1) The size of the house.

(2) The policy of the theatre.

(3) The price of the tickets. (Not only the cost of the productions, but the wealth of

the community must be taken into consideration in determining this.)
(4) The availability of operating capital.
(5) Probable percentage of capacity.

B—The budget must cover:
(1) Pre-season expenses.
   (a) Salaries.
   (b) Publicity (advertising, entertainment, office supplies, printing, mailings, phone, vehicles).
   (c) Theatre improvements and replacements.
   (d) New equipment.
   (e) Casting expenses (office space, phone, mailing).
   (f) Transportation.
   (g) Insurance.
(2) Production costs:
   (a) Salaries.
   (b) Scenery.
   (c) Lighting.
   (d) Costumes.
   (e) Props.
   (f) Royalties.
   (g) Theatre maintenance.
   (h) Publicity (advertising, entertainment, office supplies, printing, mailings, phone, photography, etc.).
   (i) Vehicles.
   (j) Insurance.
   (k) Miscellaneous. (No matter how carefully the producer plans his budget, expenses will crop up that Horatio has still never dreamed of.)
(3) Post season expenses:

(a) Salaries.
(b) Transportation.
(c) Storage.
(d) Publicity (i.e., if producer plans to open his theatre another year).
(e) Mailings (payment of final bills, unemployment slips for professional staff, income tax statements).
(f) Vehicles.
(g) Insurance.

4 Adequate housing and eating facilities at reasonable rates for resident companies.

NOTE: Housing and eating facilities may consist of anything from extremely elegant and expensive hotels and restaurants to some sort of dormitory arrangement in a company boarding house. The terms "adequate" and "reasonable" vary greatly according to the location and policy of the theatre and the salaries paid.

A—In any case there are certain unvariable requirements for decent housing accommodations. They are:
(1) Cleanliness.
(2) A comfortable bed.
(3) Toilet and bathing facilities.
(4) A reasonable amount of closet and drawer space.
(5) Reasonable proximity to theatre, i.e., within walking distance; unless management plans to provide transportation which is almost always inconvenient to both management and employee.
(6) Reasonable rates.

B—Unvariable requirements for decent eating accommodations are:
(1) Cleanliness.

(2) Well-prepared food.

(3) Possibility of a balanced diet.

(4) Reasonable proximity to theatre and living quarters.

(5) Reasonable rates.

C—The producer may then, with all of the above in mind:

(1) Check living accommodations in the area.

(2) Find out what regular rates are.

(3) Find out if his company may have reduced rates.

(4) List possibilities according to type of residence, rates, and proximity to theatre.

(5) Check restaurants in the area.

(6) List them according to rates, proximity, type of food.

D—If the producer finds the existing accommodations inadequate, he may find it necessary or advisable to make arrangements for a company boarding house. He will then:

(1) Find a house.

(2) Find someone to manage it.

(3) Find a cook.

NOTE: It is infinitely better if the owner, manager, and cook are one and the same person—or for the manager to hire his own cook.

(4) Explain to manager in no uncertain terms the absolute necessities of both housing and eating facilities. (See above.)

(5) Come to an agreement on rates:

(a) Cost of rooms, double and single.

(b) Cost of meals, by meal, week, or season.

(c) Who is to collect.

NOTE: Again, it is infinitely better for the manager of the boarding house to collect rather than having producer or anyone connected with the company do it.

> E—He will then, in all honesty and to the best of his ability, explain the living conditions and costs to every member of his company *before hiring them*. He will, if requested, make the most desirable (under the circumstances) reservations for each member of his company.
>
> F—He will transport each member of the company to his new "home" upon his arrival in town.
>
> G—He will, if he is wise, make it absolutely clear, both to the company member and the owner of the living establishment, that his responsibility ends there.

FINAL NOTE: Housing is the biggest bore and largest source of complaint that exists for most stock producers. Probably because if they had been interested in housing they would have become hotel managers or boarding-house keepers rather than theatrical producers in the first place. The most concise advice I can think of is to make sure adequate housing facilities are available, and at the same time avoid as much personal responsibility for any individual as possible.

5 A staff.

> The staff consists of all the people who will help the producer to present plays, maintain a theatre, and acquire an audience. The producer must:
>
> > A—Find the best possible person, who will fit into his budget and living conditions for each job connected with his theatre, then:

(1) Give each person as much responsibility as he can handle, *but no more*.

(2) Explain what he expects from each person and when he expects it in no uncertain terms.

(3) Allow each person to use his own intelligence, imagination, and creative ability.

(4) Never accept "creativity" as an excuse for sloppiness or laziness.

(5) Never confuse bad manners with artistic temperament.

(6) Know each person's job well enough to spot trouble the minute it arises.

(7) Be strong enough, hard-hearted enough, and wise enough to get rid of either the trouble or the person causing it. (One rotten apple, etc.)

(8) Keep reasonable check on each person's accomplishments.

(9) Give credit where it is due, but never be too easily pleased. (Best credit is offer of future work; next best is recommendation for future work. Therefore, keep names, addresses, and phone numbers of most capable people.)

(10) Have respect for his company.

(11) Not discuss the inadequacy of one member of his company with another as long as he expects them to continue working together.

(12) Behave in such a manner that his company can respect him.

(13) Not expect his company to love him. They don't anyway.

NOTE: May also read the section on casting under **The Director**.

    6 A schedule of plays.
      See section on choice of plays under THE DIRECTOR, Page 54.
    7 An audience.
      See chapters on **PUBLICITY DIRECTOR** and **PATRON'S CHAIRMAN**.

CHAPTER 22

The Property Man

The property man is the person responsible for acquiring the properties needed for each production and for returning them after the show has closed. This person is sometimes called the set decorator.

NOTE: The property man is frequently expected to "run props" during performance, but as this is a job in itself, it will be covered in a separate chapter entitled PROPERTY MANAGER.

The property man must:

1 Have taste.

    A—Be able to pick furniture, glassware, pictures, pipes, cigarette holders, bric-a-brac, luggage, etc., that will add to the beauty and authenticity of the play.

    B—Choose colors that will blend, or contrast, or do something besides clash with each other, the walls, and the leading lady's third act costume.

    C—Select furniture according to the size of the stage, i.e., it must not be so large that it dwarfs the set and hides the actors, nor so small that it looks pitiful and forlorn. (The latter is seldom a problem in small theatres.)

    D—Choose bric-a-brac that can be seen. (Otherwise it is totally useless.)

    E—Choose set decorations, furniture, and hand

props that *look* as if they fit the financial status of the characters in the play.

For example: The wealthy society hostess would never serve tea from a plastic cafeteria tray, but plated silver looks just fine—even from the first row.

2 Use common sense.

A—Find props which are practical.

Example: A beautiful sofa which cannot be sat upon—or stand up under any other business devised by the director—is useless as a prop. It should be admired, but left in the store window.

B—Prepare food props which are palatable.

Example: Actors simply cannot eat plastic grapes or drink sour milk. Cold, greasy stew is rather difficult too.

C—See that all props are *safe*.

Example: No protruding nails, no broken chair legs, no dirty dishes, no wet paint, etc.

D—Avoid extremely expensive and delicate props. (For obvious reasons.)

E—Accept the fact that a wrong prop on the stage literally paints amateur across the set in luminous paint.

3 Know something about periods and styles of furniture.

NOTE: The very young property man cannot be expected to know all about good furniture, glassware, and park bench styles of the 1700's, 1860's, 1912's, etc., but he must be willing to learn. He must be willing to accept the fact that even though two actors *can* sit on a board nailed across two barrels, this type of bench will not lend either beauty or authenticity to a Restoration comedy—even though two barrels, a board, and some nails may be very easy to come by and a 1660 bench really takes some tracking down—or some very tall ingenuity.

4 Overcome or rise above any fear or distaste he may have for asking to borrow other people's property.

5 *Before* each season begins the prop man should:

    A—Check the prop room to find out what the theatre owns.

    B—Buy himself a clip board and a pencil and a little black book—and carry them always!

    C—Find out the weekly budget for properties and plan to stay within it.

    D—Find out who lent what in previous seasons. If lists are unavailable, check credits on past programs. If possible, list type of articles lent, along with a name, address, and phone number in the little black book.

    E—Find out how theatre lists program credits.

    F—Find out if the management gives passes to property lenders. If so, get some.

    G—Find out when, where, and to whom program credits must be turned in.

    H—Find out when company truck or car is available to him.

    I—Find out where he is to get gas, and if he must have special permission to do so. (He may also do well to remember that gas, parking, etc., used for gathering props is part of the prop budget.)

    J—Get some money from business manager to cover props for first show.

    K—Find out what items are covered by insurance.

6 In order to organize his *weekly search for props,* the prop man should:

A—Read the play.

NOTE: Whenever possible this should be done before the season begins, because enough scripts are seldom available between opening night of one show and the beginning of the treasure hunt for the next one. (On manuscript plays, play brokers usually send only one script along with the sides.) The prop man will only be able to make a rough prop list from an early reading, but he will be able to absorb some of the flavor of the play, which should be helpful to him later on.

B—Schedule a meeting with the scene designer, in stock, at the same time and place each week (if possible) no later than the first day of rehearsal and preferably three or four days earlier; in community theatre, during the first rehearsal week of each production.

NOTE: At this meeting the designer should specify *exactly* what he wants in the way of furniture and set decorations. The property man *must insist* on a complete list and descriptions that he can *understand*. Otherwise, he will lose time, gasoline, shoe leather, the good will of the prospective lenders, his own spirit, and that of his coworkers. Besides he won't bring in the right props. (More prop men have been destroyed by vague designers.)

C—Schedule a meeting with the stage manager at the same time and place (each week in stock), no later than the first day of rehearsal; in community theatre, during the first rehearsal week of each production.

NOTE: At this meeting they should go over the list of hand props and set decorations and make it as complete as possible. They must both realize, however, that new props will be added during rehearsals.

D—Check the stage manager's list and the scene

designer's list for duplications and discrepancies.

E—List all the items which he knows are available on the premises. Note what must be done to make them usable.

F—List the items which must be brought in from the outside world, and where each may be obtained. Include items needed for making (E) usable.

G—Be sensible in deciding which items can be borrowed and which should be purchased.

For example: Food must always be purchased. Inexpensive glassware, pillows which can be covered and recovered, washable drapes which can be dyed and re-dyed, usually wind up being cheaper to buy than borrow.

H—Decide which items can be located by telephone and which require personal visits. This will depend partially on how good the past record of the theatre is and on the personal sales ability of the prop man. Telephone every time it seems advisable, but remember the value of personal contact when there is doubt.

I—Divide prop list into area groups to make mileage and steps count.

(1) Check important and difficult-to-get items first, e.g., three orange sofa pillows are useless if the only sofa available is red.

(2) Plan to pick up the things which must be bought in the same area where you must get particular items, i.e., dime stores may be in same area as furniture stores. When time permits, stop to get thread and typing paper

right after locating the sofa—rather than drive off in high glee at having found the sofa and then have to return three hours later (or indeed three minutes before tech rehearsal) to buy thread and typing paper.

J—Contact and deal with potential lenders.

(1) Be confident and courteous.

(a) Never be afraid to ask people to lend; remember no one minds *owning* a coveted item.

(b) Remember that no one is obligated to lend his merchandise or his personal belongings.

(c) When an item is refused, or is unavailable at the source, ask if the person knows of anyone else who may have the item; but never use the person's name without permission.

(d) Show or feign understanding to persons who cannot or will not lend.

(2) Show respect for property.

(a) List the items taken and place where they should be returned in the presence of the lender.

NOTE: A little black book for the prop man's own reference and tags which may be tied or pinned to the item are impressive and time-saving, particularly if items are to be returned by someone else. Tags may be kept in a safe place and reattached to item on strike night.

(b) Carry a blanket or other covering cloth for furniture when it is being hauled.

(c) See that breakable items are packed for safe transportation.

(d) Carry plastic bags for wrapping pillows, clothing, etc.

(e) Put properties in a specified place and see that they are covered immediately upon bringing them to the theatre.

(3) Acknowledge lenders.

(a) Find out if the lender wants program credit—and how he wants to be listed.

For example: "Edwardian sofa by the Bettis Antique Shop," *or* "Sofa courtesy of Joan Bettis."

(b) Get program credits in on time. (If an item is found too late to give credit the week of the performance in which it will be used, explain that it will be in the following week's program.)

(c) Write credits out and give them to the specified person at a specified time and place each week, in stock. Never expect anyone to carry around many little pieces of paper or remember everything (or indeed anything) he is told.

(d) Carry passes (if it is the policy of the theatre to give passes to property lenders). Give the passes when the item is promised.

(4) Return borrowed property within three days after the closing performance. (Usually the day after a new show opens is the safest time to *promise* return.)

(a) See that everything is in good condition, i.e., furniture polished, dishes clean, drapes, bed-spreads clean, etc.

(b) Tag, cover and/or pack items to be returned on strike night.

(c) See that everything is covered and/or packed well during hauling.

7 At the *end* of the season, the property man must:

A—See that the prop room is left clean and neat.

B—Return everything to its rightful owner. Check thoroughly for past mistakes.

C—Take a reasonable inventory and mark boxes.

For example: Box No. 1—cigarette holders, boxes, pipes, lighters, etc. Box No. 2—glassware. (It is not necessary to say six cheese glasses, two champagne glasses, one butter plate, etc.)

D—Turn in his final expense account, and settle all money with business manager before leaving.

E—Write thank-you notes to all the people who have been particularly helpful to him. This is never a requirement, but it certainly does pave the way for better relationships, not to mention borrowing power, for the theatre in future seasons.

CHAPTER 23

The Property Manager

The property manager is the person who is responsible for "running props" (i.e., seeing that the right prop is in the right place at the right time) during the final rehearsals and performance. The property manager must:
1. Get a complete list of every prop that is to be used in the show from the prop man or the stage manager.
2. Find out from the stage manager where each prop is to be placed.
    A—At the beginning of the show—called "at opening."
    B—During each scene and act change.
3. Note, in writing, beside each prop on the list where each prop is to be placed and for what scene.
4. Make an easy-to-check working prop sheet to *keep* and *use* from the first tech rehearsal through the final performance. Never trust the memory for this!
5. Make a new working prop sheet if the original one has so many notations on it that it is difficult to check through quickly. (See final page of this chapter for example of a simple working prop sheet.)
6. See that hand props are available by the fourth

day of rehearsal—even if the actual props have not been gathered yet.

For example: If the silver service is not ready, any *clean* tray, teapot, cups, saucers, sugar bowl, cream pitcher, spoons, napkins, and *water* may be used. (Actors simply cannot time eating and drinking scenes when all they have to swallow is air.)

7 Work with stage manager in setting up the stage from the *first* day that props are to be used in rehearsal. This usually means that the prop manager is on call at least one half hour before the rehearsal call.

8 See that all food props are palatable for rehearsals as well as performance.

    A—Check food at the end of each rehearsal or performance to see if more food must be ordered.

    B—Never wait until the last minute to get them.

    C—Wash all eating utensils before each rehearsal or performance, preferably immediately following use.

    D—Never leave dirty dishes, food, etc., overnight, through the dinner hour, etc.

    E—Remember that all of the above are always the responsibility of the property manager and no one else.

9 Strike rehearsal props and put them away at the end of rehearsal.

10 Pre-set before opening every prop that it is possible to pre-set.

For example: If a book is not used or talked about until Act III it may be placed in the shelf before opening. If a tray is brought in during Act II, but contains no perishables (such as ice or ice cream) it should be set up on prop table before opening.

11. Check to see that all props for later scenes are *ready* to be set up at designated time.
For example: Ice should be in the tray, ready to be placed in the ice bucket for Act II.
12. Have props set up at least ten minutes before the opening curtain so that they can be checked by the actors and rechecked by the stage manager.
13. Strike and/or set up props quickly and quietly—especially during scene changes.
14. Make no noise back stage.
15. Never, never, never leave anything to chance. Write and re-check everything.
16. Strike props and put them away at the end of each performance. (Common sense is necessary here; some props have to be struck; others do not.)
17. Never be afraid that absolute accuracy and complete efficiency will "look silly" or is "a waste of time."

EXAMPLE OF WORKING PROP SHEET

PROPS FOR "THE HAPPY HOUR"
July 8–13

At opening—
On desk:
  Desk set (R.)
  2 sheets paper (C.)
  Letter holder, 3 letters—open (L.)
  Ash tray (U. C.)
Bottom drawer (R.):
  Gas bill
On Bar:
  4 bottles unopened

1 scotch bottle, ½ full; open (R.)
4 high ball glasses (C.)
2 shot glasses (L.)
Cocktail napkins (D. L.)
Ash tray (D. R.)
Matches (D. R.)

On Sofa:
2 red pillows (R.)
1 green pillow (L.)
New York Times, open to sport page (R. C.)

On Coffee Table:
Cigarette box with 3 cigarettes (U. R.)
Cigarette lighter (R. C.)
Check to make sure it works!!
Bowl of pink flowers (L.)

Sofa Chair (U. C.):
Tim's glasses under cushion (R.)

Book Shelf:
Sewing basket with scissors, red thread, thimble, needle (threaded), pin cushion—third shelf from top (R.)
"Gulliver's Travels"—bottom shelf (L.)
Bowl of ivy on doiley—top shelf (C.)

Window Sill (R.):
Potted plant (C.)

Off Left Prop Table:
Tea tray with 3 cups and saucers, 3 spoons, 1 tea pot, sugar bowl with lump sugar, tongs, cream pitcher (empty), cream for pitcher

By Door:
Blue luggage including train case, suit case, hat box

Off Right Prop Table:
Flower basket, yellow flowers, garden gloves, garden shears

Personal:
    Tim—Telegram in pocket of brown jacket
    Jane—Car keys in black purse

PROPS FOR "THE HAPPY HOUR"
July 8–13
Act I—*Scene 2*

Strike from coffee table—Pink flowers
Set up on coffee table—Yellow flowers
Strike from end table (u. c.)—Sewing basket
Set up on bookshelf—Sewing basket, 3rd shelf from top (c.)

Act II

Strike from sofa—2 red pillows, *New York Times*
Set up on sofa—2 flowered pillows (R.), book—"Gullivers Travels" (C.)
Strike from C.—Blue luggage
Set up (*Off* R.) for Act III—Blue luggage

Act III

Strike from desk—Letters
Strike from bookshelf—Sewing basket
Set up on bookshelf—Oil painting set—brush, easel cloth, several colors of paint
Strike from coffee table—Cards
Set up on coffee table—Tea tray
    Check: 3 cups and saucers, spoons, sugar bowl and tongs, cream pitcher (empty), 1 teapot (u. R.)
Check off (R.)—Blue luggage—train case, suit case
Check off (L.)—Cream for pitcher
Personal
    Ellen—Letter in brown purse
    Joe—Contract in pocket of tweed jacket
    Tim—Glasses in pocket of blue coat
Strike all used glasses. Wash and replace on bar. Empty all ash trays.

CHAPTER **24**

The Publicity Director

The publicity director is the person responsible for generating enough interest in enough people to fill the house fairly regularly with paying customers. He must:

1. Remember that he is representing a place of business and dress accordingly. Gone are the days of the sloppy press agent. No more need be said on this subject.
2. Take full advantage of any opportunity for free space:

    A—Make the rounds; get to know the newpaper editors personally.

    B—Never underestimate the intelligence or the power of a newspaper editor.

    (1) Listen to his suggestions; he usually knows his readers pretty well.

    (2) Write honest releases.

    (3) Never demand space or make scenes when releases are not used.

    (4) *Find out the most convenient time for editor to receive weekly releases.*

    (5) Find out whether newspapers prefer to receive 8 x 10 photographs, negatives, special sized photographs, or newspaper cuts or mats.

NOTE: Most small newspapers do not have engravers. Photographs must be sent out. The publicity man who expects to have pictures printed in the paper must arrange to have the cuts made in time to include them with his release. Cuts usually cost about five dollars each and should be included in the advertising budget.

The most common and expensive error made by new press agents is to load newspaper offices with 8 x 10 photographs which the paper has neither the time nor the money to have made into cuts.

    (6) Keep card files (and refer to them) on what each paper will use, has used, kind of pictures wanted, deadline dates for releases, and *NAMES* of editors, drama editors, etc. Never assume that all newspapers or newspaper men are alike!

    (7) Write general releases early, at least three or four days before deadline.

NOTE: Enough midnight oil must be burned in getting out specials that come up at the last minute.

    (8) Avoid a constant rush to meet the deadline because the following will undoubtedly result and are absolutely taboo.

        (a) Untidy copy.
        (b) Incorrect spelling.
        (c) Faulty punctuation.
        (d) Carbon copies.

NOTE: Carbon copies are for theatre files only! General releases may be mimeographed. Special releases *must* be individually typed.

    (9) Set deadline for releases to be mimeographed or typed, envelopes to be addressed, stuffed, and stamped.

    (10) Mail releases to editor or drama ed-

itor. Never enclose them with advertising copy.

(11) Mail releases on time, but not so early that they will be lost in the shuffle.

(12) Never be afraid to show personal interest and appreciation for newspaper men.

(13) Never become a pest by hanging around a newspaper office too much.

NOTE: Remember newspaper men have other work to do, no matter how much they love the theatre (and they usually do!) or how helpful they want to be (and they usually do!).

C—Remember that the best publicity does not come from the pen of the publicity director, but from reporters, columnists, society editors, feature writers, and drama editors of the newspapers themselves.

(1) Arrange to meet as many newspaper men and women as possible.

(2) Try to incite their interest in the theatre.

(3) Suggest angles for stories.

(4) Ask them for suggestions for special stories.

(5) Offer co-operation in arranging for interviews, photographs, information.

(6) Always keep appointments.

(7) Never attempt to write the story for a writer.

D—Use individual common-sense method in dealing with radio and T.V. personnel; they too are both intelligent and powerful.

3 Use his advertising budget wisely.

A—Determine the possible gross receipts.

Handbook for Theatrical Apprentices

B—Plan to spend about ten per cent of the possible gross on advertising.

NOTE: In the case of a new theatre, new management, or other special conditions, this figure may be raised, but never without specific orders from the producer.

C—Find out the name and circulation of daily and weekly newspapers in the area.

NOTE: This information can be obtained from *Editor's and Press Agents Year Book,* if unavailable through local sources.

D—Find out the cost of advertising space in each paper. (Cost on small dailies and weeklies is usually little.)

E—Remember the value of good will which may be gained from advertising in local weeklies and dailies—even though the circulation is not large.

F—Design the basic ad:

(1) (a) A signature cut (or slug) which is unique and easily recognizable.

(b) The *same shape* each week.

(c) The same size each week (unless it is changed for a particular purpose).

(d) The same days of each week.

(e) The same space (i.e., page and column number each week).

NOTE: Newspapers will usually co-operate if ads are set up in advance for a reasonable length of time.

(2) Give necessary information. Always include:

(a) The name of the theatre.

(b) The location of the theatre.

(c) The box office phone number.

(d) The special or local phone number where reservations may be made.

NOTE: This usually differs for each newspaper. Double check it!

    (e) The curtain time.
    (f) The playing dates.
    (g) The title of the play.
    (h) The star's name (if any).

WARNING: Stars and feature players have clauses in their contracts denoting placement of their names, size and boldness of print. Their billing must be right in every respect.

NOTE: Actors in resident companies can sometimes be built into local "stars" with the right help from the publicity director.

   (3) Avoid cluttered ads.
    G—Have cuts made of slug and a, b, c, d, e at the beginning of the session.
    H—Fill in f, g, h weekly or for each production.
    I—Find out weekly deadline for advertising copy for each newspaper.
    J—Determine own deadline for completing ad each week including addressing, stuffing, and stamping envelopes.

NOTE: Make sure picture cuts are enclosed with copy (if pictures are to be used in ads).

    K—Mail copy on time.

NOTE: The above rules concerning basic information accuracy, familiarity, and promptness apply to radio and T.V. spots too.

 4 Use each theatre program as a means of promotion.
   A—The program provides valuable advertising because it reaches a captive audience.
    (1) People who are already interested in theatre.

(2) People who already know where the theatre is.

(3) People who have time (before the curtain and at intermission) to read copy.

(4) People who are among other people who are reading the same thing.

(5) People who are already near the box office.

B—An effective theatre program consists of:

(1) An attractive and distinguishable cover.

(2) At least enough paid advertising to cover cost of printing.

(3) An eye catching advertisement of the next production (preferably on the first page).

(4) A schedule of the season's productions including playing dates (preferably on last page).

(5) Masthead for THIS WEEK'S SHOW (preferably on center pages):

    (a) Name of theatre.
    (b) Producers.
    (c) Stars.
    (d) Title of play.
    (e) Author of play.
    (f) Feature players.
    (g) Director.
    (h) Scene designer.
    (i) Lighting designer.

WARNING: Though the above is the usual order, the publicity director *must* check contracts for correct billing in respect to name placement, size of print, and boldness of type for all personnel.

KIND ADVICE: The publicity director who SPELLS

NAMES INCORRECTLY SHOULD FOLD HIS TENT, and quietly steal away. It's better that way.

(6) Synopsis of scenes—

Example:

ACT I—SCENE 1

Living room of the Biddle Smith's on Long Island on a fall morning in 1860.

SCENE 2

Central Park, New York City on a spring afternoon, 1861.

INTERMISSION—15 Minutes.

ACT II—SCENE 1

The Biddle Smith's on a summer night, 1861.

SCENE 2

The Biddle Smith's, the following morning.

(7) Cast in order of appearance.

Example:

CHARACTER'S NAME .... *Actor's Name*
CHARACTER'S NAME .... *Actor's Name*

NOTE: Information for (6) and (7) should be obtained from stage manager on first day of rehearsal.

(8) Who's Who in cast.

(a) Who's Who may remain the same each week for resident company, and may appear on permanent pages.

(b) Space on change sheets must be used for Who's Who of prominent jobbers.

(c) Obviously Who's Who must change weekly for star or package companies.

(9) Listing of the theatre's permanent staff.

Example:

PRODUCER .... *Joe Blow*
MANAGING DIRECTOR .... *John Doe*
PRODUCTION STAGE MANAGER .... *Jack Sprat*

Etc. down to and including apprentices. A large staff

looks impressive to the public, and some staff members want and frequently need a printed record of their work.

    (10) Who's Who of staff members. (Not necessary, but advisable, because it helps public to feel that they know the company and are a part of the theatre. These Who's Whos may appear on permanent pages of program and are therefore, not expensive.)

    (11) Pictures!!

        (a) Photographs with each Who's Who help public to identify and remember actors and staff. They are particularly important for actors.

        (b) Photographs of the next production or leading players stimulate interest.

        (c) One or more new pictures on each program add interest.

NOTE: *Write as much program copy in advance as possible. Who's Who, for example, may be written as soon as each member of cast or staff is set. Too much last minute work leads toward dull program copy.*

5 Use mailings to create personal interest in and awareness of the theatre.

    A—Obtain mailing lists early since it is literally impossible to form complete and effective lists during the season. Possible sources of information are:

        (1) Mailing lists of previous seasons.

        (2) Local chamber of commerce.

        (3) Local or neighboring community theatres.

        (4) Local concert series chairmen.

        (5) Local literary clubs.

B—Plan number, kind, and timing of mailings carefully in order to reach largest number of possible and probable ticket buyers.

C—Set deadline for:
  (1) Writing material for mailings.
  (2) Getting material to printers (or mimeographer).
  (3) Addressing envelopes.
  (4) Getting material back from printers.
  (5) Stuffing envelopes.
  (6) Putting mailings in the mail.

D—See that each mailing includes:
  (1) Name of theatre.
  (2) Location of theatre.
  (3) Box-office phone number.
  (4) Playing dates.
  (5) Ticket prices.
  AND
  (6) At least one item of special interest (i.e., reason for the mailing) such as:
    (a) Schedule of plays.
    (b) Theatre party plan.
    (c) Subscription plan.
    (d) List of stars.
    (e) Announcement of a particular play.
    (f) Hold-overs.
    (g) Change in schedule.
    (h) Thanks for something.

6 Use gimmick publicity stunts only when they can be planned in detail and followed through with professional aplomb.

NOTE: Nothing is more embarrassing than a scraggy parade, a benefit singer who can't sing, a tacky window display, etc.

7 Take advantage of opportunities to display actor's pictures, theatrical pictures, theatre schedules, etc. in an attractive manner.

    A—Get permission for displays from proprietors of public places, such as:
        (1) Banks.
        (2) Hotels and motels.
        (3) Restaurants.
        (4) Bars.
        (5) Night clubs.
        (6) Movie theatres.
        (7) Schools.
        (8) Stores.
        (9) Libraries.
    B—Design attractive displays.
    C—Collect material for displays.
    D—Make arrangements to have building, painting, pasting, etc., done by specified personnel at a specified time.

NOTE: More perfectly good promotion material has been left in offices and the back seats of cars, because publicity directors had neither the time nor inclination to build, paint, paste, etc., and had simply never assigned these tasks to qualified people.

    E—Display displays!
    F—Arrange to change displays often enough to keep them interesting—but not so often that publicity director has no time for anything else.
        (1) New pictures.
        (2) New titles.
        (3) New dates.

NOTE: See (D). This rule holds true for changes too.

8 Use complimentary tickets wisely.

    A—Arrange for all free passes to be given for

opening night or preview performances so that passes serve not only as "thank yous" but as "word of mouth" publicity.

B—Carefully plan invitation lists for any "by invitation only" performances. File for future.

NOTE: Many summer theatres have a special Grand Opening or Preview Performance for an invited audience. Invitation lists may include any or all of the following, according to the number of people wanted:

(1) Personnel from local newspapers, radio and television stations.

(2) Those who have been particularly helpful to the theatre:
  (a) Advisory board.
  (b) Patron ticket sellers.
  (c) Frequent lenders of props, costumes, etc.
  (d) Local jobbers from other seasons.
  (e) Program advertisers.
  (f) Personal friends of the management.

(3) Those who can be helpful in the future:
  (a) City officials.
  (b) Prominent merchants or business men.
  (c) Prominent club men or women.
  (d) Presidents of Chambers of Commerce.
  (e) Producers of other theatres.

9 Keep complete scrapbook of printed publicity.
10 Keep complete accounts of all moneys spent on publicity.
11 Turn expense accounts over to business manager weekly at specified time and place.

CHAPTER 25

The Scene Designer

The scene designer is the person responsible for planning the stage set or settings for each production and for the final painting, i.e., art work on the set. He must:
1 Be aware of the physical plant in which he and his crew will work.

   A—Know his stage dimensions:
   (1) Size of proscenium (if any).
   (2) Depth of stage.
   (3) Wing space, right and left.
   (4) Height.
      (a) Fly space (if any).
      (b) Lines available (if any).
   (5) Storage space.

   And if he is exceedingly lucky:
   (6) Turn tables.
   (7) Treadmills.
   (8) Other special advantages.

   And if he is exceedingly unlucky:
   (9) Disadvantages:
      (a) Poles center stage.
      (b) Rafters or beams rear of stage.
      (c) Bad sight lines.

   B—Check his stock pile for size and condition:
   (1) Flats.
   (2) Platforms.
   (3) Stair units.

135

(4) Door units.
(5) Window units.
(6) Columns, pedestals, balustrades, railings, etc.
(7) Ceiling.

C—Check his tool supply.

NOTE: This should be done in co-ordination with the technical director. Imagination, skill, ingenuity are of the essence and have performed near miracles, but no T.D. can build units for which he is completely and totally unequipped. A scene designer simply must bear this in mind.

D—Check his paint supply and order at least enough whiting, glue, wheat paste, brushes, etc., to work at least two shows ahead.

E—Check his supply of fabrics:
(1) Draperies.
(2) Slipcovers.
(3) Cushions and cushion covers.
(4) Rugs.

F—Check his supply of theatre-owned props and furniture.

G—Check stores and theatrical supply houses in area.
(1) Know what is available.
(2) Know approximate cost.
(3) Plan sets accordingly.

Example: Burnt orange satin brocaded drapes, 30 feet wide and 12 feet high are simply not to be had in some areas. Better plan a substitute or order them way, way, way in advance. P.S. Include cost of delivery in budget.

2 Determine his budget (which is, after all, an intricate part of the physical plant).

A—Plan to work under budget whenever possible, because no matter how carefully he plans, *some* items will cost more than he expected.

B—Plan to use available stock pile and supplies whenever possible without seriously damaging final set.

C—Keep careful account of where, when and how all money is spent.

(1) Get receipts for every purchase.

(2) Keep account books for himself.

(3) Turn expense account in to business manager weekly at specified time and place.

3 Buy the scripts and read them in advance. (Not necessary, but helpful.)

A—Most scripts, by the time they are released for stock or community productions, are available in paperback editions.

B—Original investment can usually be added to weekly expense account.

C—When plays are obtained in manuscript, much consternation is avoided in not having to wait his turn for the one master script which play brokers usually send along with sides.

D—Considerable money is saved in the long run on tranquilizers, aspirin tablets, and trips to the post office.

4 Draw a rough sketch of floor plan for each production and have it approved by director *at least* one or two days before rehearsal.

5 Keep in mind the fact that a set must work for the play, the director, and the performers as well as look attractive.

6 Make complete renderings of the set and turn it over to the technical director by the first rehearsal. Renderings should include:

A—List of items to be used from stock pile.
B—Complete plans for new set pieces.
  (1) Scale drawings.
  (2) Type of lumber to be used.
  (3) Covering, such as muslin, canvas, velour.
  (4) Special material such as chicken wire, plaster, casters, glitter dust, etc., etc., etc.
  (5) Colors for base coats of paint.
C—Water color sketch of final set or settings.
  (1) Every T.D. works better if he knows what the final result is expected to look like.
  (2) Costumier cannot work at all without knowing colors.
  (3) The prop man or set decorator cannot choose furniture or set dressings without knowing placement and colors.

NOTE: It is easier to change a paint color than the leading lady's only evening dress or the furniture store's only five foot sofa.

D—Plans for changing scenery if more than one set is needed.
  (1) Storage space for unused items.
  (2) Ways and means of setting up and striking sets.
E—Plans for backings, off-stage exits from platforms.

7 Build a model set *when time allows*.

WARNING: Time will not allow unless much work is done in advance and sufficient technical help is available. If short cuts must be made, let the model set be the first to go.

8 Make a complete list of furniture and set dressings, including rugs, drapes, pictures, flowers, etc.

    A—Set time and place to meet with prop man weekly no later than first day of rehearsal.
    B—Go over each item carefully. Make sure he understands exactly what he is to get.
    C—Whenever possible, pick his own furniture, drapes, etc.
    D—Check props as they are brought in.
9. Co-ordinate plans with stage manager for changing scenery, at least two days before dress rehearsal.
10. Mix paint for final painting.
11. Finish as much of the set as possible *before* it goes up.
12. Add finishing touches of paint as soon as set goes up. (A well-planned set should be finished by tech rehearsal; however, floor painting may have to wait until after dress rehearsal—immediately after. Nothing is more difficult for a performer than trying to appear graceful on a wet, slippery floor.)
13. Supervise the set dressing.
14. Check set under lights at dress rehearsal and make necessary revisions, which should be slight.

NOTE: Sometimes a scene designer is expected to or insists upon lighting his own sets. **CHAPTER 16 deals with THE LIGHTING DESIGNER.**

CHAPTER 26

The Secretary

The Secretary is the person who is responsible *to his boss* for correspondence, i.e., communication by phone, letter, telegram, carrier pigeon, gift, or personal interview. He must:

1 Find out who his boss is and take orders from him alone. The boss may give him specific duties for other personnel such as:

   A—Before Friday the *stage manager* will give you the mast head for next week's program. Type it and mail it to the printers.

   B—On Tuesday mornings the *Publicity Director* will give you material for releases. Find out how many copies he wants; type them and send them to the places he lists for you. He will also give you material for the program; send it along to the printers too. Friday is the deadline.

   C—Check with the *business manager* each morning to see if he has any letters or checks to be typed.

   D—Get a list from the *prop man* of places where couches may be available. Call each one and find out if we may borrow one, and if not how much it will cost to rent. Be sure to find out when we can pick it up, and let prop man know.

E—Check with the *director* and find out whom he wants to see for that bit in the third show. Find out when he wants to read people and set up appointments.

F—Wire the *play brokers;* tell them they neglected to send the *leading man's* sides along with the others; ask them to send them immediately. Please. He only has the longest part since Hamlet.

G—Bring me coffee.

H—When you get a chance, stop in and talk to *Mrs. Regular Patron. Miss Star* forgot to thank her for the flowers she sent opening night. Soothe her. YOU KNOW.

I—Make mimeographed copies of the additions to the script. *The author* will give them to you. Have them ready tomorrow morning. It's only five o'clock now. YOU can make it.

J—*Mr. Backer* wants to see the show Friday night. See that he has four good seats. Better call a good restaurant and make reservations for dinner too.

K—My *mother's* birthday is the 6th of next month. Remind me. Better yet just wire flowers. Say I'm thinking of her.

L—Bring me coffee.

M—Call Joe's Place and tell them to send coffee and sandwiches up for the whole cast on dress rehearsal.

N—Bring me coffee.

NOTE: This list of duties may sound contradictory to the secretary's first rule (which is, I repeat, to find out who his boss is and take orders from him alone). It isn't. It merely points out that the boss will undoubtedly give the secretary enough jobs to keep him busy from morning until night—at least. If the secretary offers his services to others he will find himself doing everything from typing new sides for a spoiled apprentice, who "left-them-in-his-Jaguar-when-he-took-it-to-the-garage-that-morning," to writing love notes to the leading man's seven girl friends and "don't-mix-them-up-for-lord's-sake."

2 Keep his office in order.

    A—See that he is supplied at all times with necessary supplies such as steno pads, scratch paper, stationery, envelopes, copy paper, carbon paper, fountain pens, paper clips, staples, typewriter ribbons, stamps, etc.

    B—Keep telephone books handy.

    C—Keep often-called numbers handy.

    D—See that typewriters, mimeo machines, etc. are kept in good repair.

    E—Know how to run them.

3 Know the basic rules for any secretary and follow them.

    A—Be neat.

    B—Be quick.

    C—Be accurate.

    D—Be prompt.

    E—Be polite.

And it also helps to:

    F—Be charming.

4 Keep complete account of all expenses and turn them in to business manager at a specified time and place each week.

5 Learn to anticipate the boss's needs.

NOTE: A good secretary cannot be a robot, but must frequently use his own judgment and his own imagination.

CHAPTER 27

The Sound Technician

The sound technician is the person responsible for the execution of sound effects (excluding live music) for a production. He must:
1 Be responsible for the preparation and care of sound equipment.
    A—Check (or have the electrician check) the safety of his equipment.
    B—Check his machine (there are many kinds). Make sure it is in good working order, i.e., turn tables, needle, volume control, speakers, etc.
    C—Check other sound equipment. Make sure it is in good working order, i.e., microphones, tape recorder, door bells, telephone bells, and whatever.
    D—Be able to diagnose defects in sound equipment.
        (1) Make minor repairs.
        (2) Call in a professional repair man when necessary.
    E—Find out what sources are available for obtaining additional equipment or parts.
        (1) Borrowing for how long.
        (2) Renting, approximate cost.
        (3) Buying, approximate cost.
    F—Determine what new equipment is necessary.

143

144 Handbook for Theatrical Apprentices

G—Determine what new equipment is desirable.

NOTE: Remember the budget.

H—Have business manager or producer verify orders for new equipment.

I—Order new equipment immediately upon verification.

(1) Not wait until air express shipment is necessary.

(2) Not wait until valuable time and energy must be wasted planning and preparing substitutes, "just in case" equipment does not arrive on time.

J—Remember that almost all sound equipment is delicate.

(1) Never let novices handle it unless supervised.

(2) Keep it clean, dry, covered.

(3) *Turn it off* when not in use.

NOTE: *Volume turned down does not count!*

K—Check record supply, if any.

(1) List what he has in stock.

(2) Separate scratchy, cracked, and otherwise defective records. Report to management.

L—Find out what sources are available for obtaining (borrowing, buying, renting, taping) additional records:

(1) Local radio stations.

(2) Local record shops.

(3) New York companies.

(4) Play brokers.

M—Return borrowed or rented equipment within two days after final performance.

(1) See that it is clean and in good condition.

(2) Pack it correctly for shipping (if necessary).

N—Never hold equipment for use in future shows without owner's permission.

O—Keep strict account of money spent on sound equipment and effects. Give expense account to business manager weekly at specified time and place.

2 Prepare sound plot and equipment for each production.

A—Read the play.

NOTE: Sound technicians, like everyone else connected with the production, will profit by doing this in advance.

B—Find out from the director what kind of sound effects he wants, i.e., live or recorded —symphony, band, piano.

NOTE: The director may know the exact record he wants, or he may just know the type of effect he wants to get.

C—*Write* notes as given by director.

D—Bear in mind the available equipment and plan to use in the following order:

(1) Theatre-owned.

(2) From near-by sources.

(3) Other sources.

E—Get records or other sound effect equipment as designated by director and/or indicated by script.

NOTE: If sound technician is unsure, he will be wise to provide several selections for director to choose from.

F—If special recordings must be cut of actor's voices, street noises, water bubbling, or anything else, make the recording early in the rehearsal period.

(1) Make appointments for making cuts.

(2) Have equipment ready at designated time.

G—Be ready to test sound effects as designated in (B) with the director at least two days before tech rehearsal, so there will be time to make necessary corrections.

H—Mark the part of the record to be used with tape as soon as it is tested.

(1) Never trust the memory.

(2) If more than one part of a particular record is to be used, mark each tape 1, 2, 3, etc. from the outside in.

I—Note on a sheet of paper on a clip board:

(1) Name of the record.

(2) The marking number.

(3) The approximate volume.

(4) The act, scene, page, and probable line cue.

J—Transfer notes to another sheet of paper in order of use.

(1) Type when possible or at least print legibly.

(2) Always leave space between each cue for corrections or new cues.

K—Turn prepared live sound equipment over to stage manager.

NOTE: If special handling is necessary for door bells, guns shots, etc., *explain*.

L—Provide something to cover important sound effects if mechanical equipment fails.

For example: A cover gun *plus* a board to slam on the floor for gun shot; a suspended pipe to be struck with a hammer for door bell, etc. *Explain*.

M—*If* tape is to be used during performance, transfer sounds to tape *before* tech rehearsal.

N—*If* disks are to be used during performance, keep them sorted, so that they can be easily identified and reached during tech rehearsal.

3 Test all sound effects with the action during tech rehearsal. (By tomorrow isn't soon enough.)

A—Take warns and cues from stage manager.

B—Take time to number each sound effect.

Example: ACT I, Sc. 1.

No. 1—Name of record, no. of marking, turntable used.

Warn cue *Up*.

Cue *Up*.

(Mark whether it is fade in slow, fast, sudden and exact volume.)

Warn *Out*.

(Mark whether it is a fade out slow, fast or sudden.)

No. 2—Name of record . . . etc.

C—Set up each sound effect in advance according to the number of turntables available.

Example: If two turntables are available set up No. 1 and No. 2, on turntables A and B. As soon as No. 1 is finished, set up No. 3 on turntable A. As soon as No. 2 is finished, set up No. 4 on turntable B, etc.

NOTE: Of course if one theme record is used often and several others are used at reasonably long intervals, it is advisable to leave the theme record on turnable A and simply keep changing records on turntable B.

D—Be sure to turn machine on far enough in advance of each cue to have it warmed up sufficiently for the sound (and not just the machine) to be heard on cue.

E—Never make any additional sounds—unless the sound booth is absolutely sound proof.

NOTE: Imagine the distraction when the heroine says "Now, I'm all alone. Everyone else on the island is dead," and at that moment a coke bottle rolls across the floor.

F—Make notes as the director gives them. *Never trust the memory.*

G—Make corrections according to notes.

H—Correct the cue sheet.

NOTE: If many changes have been made, make a new, neat, and easy-to-follow cue sheet.

I—Put cue sheet up in a place where it is easy to see. (No fumbling papers.)

J—Remove (or put out of the way) *all* unused records, equipment, and assorted junk.

K—Check booth before leaving.

(1) Machine should be *turned off* and closed or covered.

(2) All equipment should be in its proper place.

4 Run the sound for dress rehearsal as a performance according to the corrected cue sheet, following instructions for tech rehearsal.

A—Set up and check all sound equipment at least one half hour before scheduled curtain time.

B—Remember that timing is of the utmost importance. A sound cue even seconds too late or too early can ruin an entire scene.

C—Never "jar" the audience by making sounds too loud or abrupt *unless* for a specific purpose according to the director's orders.

D—Stay on the job. Missed sound cues are simply out of the question.

E—Take final notes as given by director after dress rehearsal.

F—Make technical and cue sheet adjustments according to director's notes.

5 Run each and every performance according to final cue sheet, taking cues and warnings from stage manager.

6 Remember that his job is not complete until he has:

A—Taken final inventory of equipment at end of season.

B—Given one copy to stage manager.

NOTE: Play safe, keep a copy.

C—Returned every borrowed or rented item.

D—Stored theatre owned equipment correctly for out-of-season protection.

E—Turned in final expense accounts.

CHAPTER **28**

The Stage Manager

The stage manager is the person who is responsible for *everything, except* the individual performances of the actors, that takes place on stage or back stage during each performance and during the rehearsal period.

1 Make initial preparations for the physical production of the play *before the first rehearsal*.

    A—Mark the stage floor or rehearsal space according to the exact measurements of the floor plan (or plans) of the scene designer.

NOTE: In case of several sets, the stage manager may mark set No. 1 with white tape, set No. 2 with orange tape, etc.

    B—Make sure there are enough chairs (folding chairs will do), tables, etc., to set up a reasonable facsimile of each set.

        (1) Set up first scene with pseudo furniture.

        (2) Never use actual prop furniture until specified by director.

        (3) Never use prop furniture of current show as rehearsal furniture for next production.

    C—Find out from designer what type of furniture and set decorations are to be used.

        (1) Type the list (or print legibly).

        (2) Give one copy of the list to prop man.

        (3) Keep one copy.

D—Check with technical director to see that he has:
- (1) Sufficient help.
- (2) Sufficient equipment.
- (3) Complete set renderings.
- (4) Deadline for completion.

E—Check the script for a basic prop list.
- (1) Type the list (or print legibly).
- (2) Give one copy to prop man.
- (3) Keep one copy.
- (4) Designate deadline for prop delivery.

NOTE: Most master scripts have a master prop list in the back made out by the stage manager of the original production of the show. These are most helpful, but should be checked over carefully.

- (5) Delete props not to be used in the present production.
- (6) Add new props designated by director and scene designer.

Of course, if it is an original script, the stage manager must read the script and make his own prop list. He is a kind gentleman and a scholar indeed if he includes this lists in the master script for the stage manager of future productions.

F—Check with costumier to see if he has:
- (1) A basic costume plot.
- (2) Sufficient help.
- (3) Sufficient equipment.
- (4) Deadline for delivery.

G—Get the cast list from the director.
- (1) Type the list (or print legibly).
- (2) Post one copy on call board.
- (3) Keep one copy.

H—Post the rehearsal schedule.
- (1) Time and place of first rehearsal.

(2) Daily rehearsal schedule.

(3) Performance dates and times.

NOTE: In one-a-week stock the schedule may be the same each week. If so, one schedule posted at the beginning of the season may be sufficient, except for special calls.

    I—Assign (and post) duties to apprentices and/or assistants.

NOTE: A stage manager cannot be expected to assign and explain specific chores, but to assign each apprentice to a job such as assistant to the technical director, prop man, electrician, costumier, etc. The apprentice is then responsible to immediate supervisor, i.e., *Boss*. This must be made absolutely clear to said apprentice or assistant.

    J—*Assign specific duties and responsibilities to the assistant stage manager!*

NOTE: Every stage manager has the prerogative of deciding these for himself.

    K—Give scripts or sides to each member of the cast.

NOTE: This is sometimes done at the beginning of the first rehearsal.

2 Prepare his master script *during rehearsal period*.

    A—Write the block (i.e., stage directions) in the book:

        (1) For each member of the cast.

        (2) As it is given by the director.

        (3) Next to the line on which actor is to do the business.

        (4) Lightly, with a pencil.

    B—Make changes in the script if director changes blocking or business.

    C—Make a list of each prop and where it is used first.

    D—Keep separate list of new props as indicated

by director and make sure they are added to prop man's list.

E—Make list of costume notes, if special things come up that have not been included in costume plot.

For Example: Costume plot may call for an apron; director may ask actress to put something in apron pocket. Make sure costumier knows that apron must have a pocket —before dress rehearsal.

F—Mark each light cue and warn as it is given by director. (Lightly, please, until actual lighting is set.)

NOTE: If special notes are given such as colors, areas, or equipment, write these on a separate page on clipboard indicating Act, Scene, Page, Line. Reserve for discussion with electrician.

G—Mark each sound cue and warn as it is given by director. (Lightly, please, until actual sound is set.)

NOTE: If special notes are given in rehearsal as to records to be used, volume, cross fades, special sound effects, etc., write these on a sheet of paper on clip-board indicating Act, Scene, Page. Reserve for discussion with sound technician.

H—Cross out or write in any changes in dialogue as indicated by director. (Again, write lightly, please, until changes are definite.)

I—Mark warns for curtains and whether curtains should be fast, slow, steady.

3 Conduct rehearsals.

A—See that rehearsal area is kept clean.

B—Set up stage before each scene. (For first rehearsal call of each day, the scene should be set *before the time* that actors are called.)

C—Place butt cans in strategic places.

D—Give rehearsal calls.

  (1) Posted daily calls are helpful especially for large-cast shows with various people in each scene.

  (2) Call actors to places after stage is set and checked.

  (3) Ditto on props when props are to be used.

  (4) Give special calls for pictures, costume fittings, interviews, and whatever, as far in advance as possible. (*Post.*)

E—"Stay with" the book, i.e., keep close enough watch on the book to:

  (1) Call out any mistakes in blocking.

  (2) Feed lines to each actor the moment he needs them.

   (a) Usually it is best to wait until the actor asks for a line.

   (b) Stop the actor if he skips an important section of dialogue.

   (c) Mark it lightly in the script or on clip-board if actor juxtaposes words, leaves out phrases, or adds his own during rehearsals.

   (d) Remind actors of mistakes during a break.

   (e) Cue an actor with a key word or phrase, never long "expressive" speeches.

   (f) Mark pauses in the script.

4 Check regularly with each department head to see that each phase of production is up-to-date—if not, why not, and what must be done to remedy the situation.

A—Give new notes, as taken in rehearsal, to each department head.

B—Check progress on original demands.

C—See that basic plots—for lights, scene changes, props, etc. are being written or typed.

D—See that front curtains, fly lines, etc. are in working order.

5 Organize scene shifts, i.e., let each member of the crew know exactly what is expected of him during each scene change.

NOTE: If scene changes are complicated, the scene shift plot should be typed (or printed legibly) and posted, *and* rehearsed without the presence of actors.

6 Give warns and cues to staff during technical rehearsal:

A—Stage crew, including property manager.

B—Electrician.

C—Sound technician.

D—Members of the cast (by scene only).

7 Take time to check accuracy of all technical phases of production, and to fully mark master script when each warn and cue is definitely set.

NOTE: Some stage managers prefer to mark light cues in blue, sound in red, curtains in black, etc. This is up to the discretion of the individual stage manager. The only specific rule is that a well marked book be perfectly clear to anyone, who, for one reason or another, has to "take over" and run the show.

8 Give call for next rehearsal, stating whether it is to be another tech rehearsal, a line rehearsal, spot scene rehearsal, or full dress rehearsal, before dismissing anyone from tech rehearsal.

9 Run dress rehearsal.

A—See that stage and back stage areas are clean.

B—Have stage completely set by half hour.

C—Double check everything during half hour.

D—Call "half hour," "ten minutes," and "places," at each dressing room before the show.

E—Check to see that actors are, or can be, ready before taking the curtain.

   (1) Impress actors with the necessity of being ready on time.

   (2) Never take curtain without checking to see that actors are there.

F—Warn on-stage actors before taking the curtain.

G—*Follow book.*

   (1) Give warns and cues to technicians—lights, sound, scenery, etc.—as designated in tech rehearsal.

   (2) Never feed lines unless absolutely necessary.

   (3) Mark mistakes lightly in book.

   (4) Remind actors of mistakes at the end of rehearsal (not at intermission).

H—Take a timing on each scene, scene change, act.

I—Call "five minutes" and "places" during intermission.

J—Take curtain calls after final curtain, making it absolutely clear that *no* actor is excused until he is dismissed by the stage manager.

K—Give calls for next rehearsal or performance.

   (1) State time of rehearsal.

   (2) State kind of rehearsal—line. spot scene, technical, or full dress.

(3) Tell actors and technicians where and when notes will be given by director.

L—See that props are put away, and furniture covered after curtain calls.

10 See that technical mistakes made in dress rehearsal are corrected before opening.

A—Take all technical notes as given by director —even though each department head takes his own notes.

B—Check with each department head to see that he knows what has to be done, and that he has (or gets) sufficient help and equipment to accomplish it in time.

11 Run every show according to rules for dress rehearsal, and in addition:

A—Note any damages to set, props, costumes, etc. during each performance.

B—See that department heads are aware of damages and that repairs are made before the following performance.

12 Organize and direct strike night.

A—Collect scripts and sides.

(1) Erase markings in manuscripts.

(2) Mail manuscripts to play broker.

B—Give definite chores to each person who is to assist on strike night.

(1) Costumier (with assistant if assigned) strikes costumes from stage area immediately after last curtain. Collects other costumes from dressing rooms and marks them for return, cleaning, or packing.

(2) Prop man (with assistant or prop manager) strikes props from stage area immediately after last curtain; collects other props, cleans them, covers them, marks them for

return, puts them in a safe place until return can be made, or puts them away if they are theatre property.

(3) Crew members may be assigned the following specific tasks:

(a) Raise ceiling.

(b) Bring tools to stage area.

(c) Pull dutchmen (roll and put away).

(d) Pull flats, put on edge of stage for stripping, put stage braces in designated place.

(e) Pull platforms, put on edge of stage for stripping.

(f) Strip flats and platforms.

NOTE: Stage manager must designate to what degree they must be stripped, i.e., hinges off or on, doors and windows left in or taken out of frames, brackets for curtain rods off or on, carpeting on platforms off or on. In any case protruding nails must be removed.

(g) Strip lumber and sort it.

(h) Tote and fetch, i.e., in summer stock and repertory, tote old scenery and lumber back to scene dock or shop; fetch new scenery to stage area.

(i) Store used scenery in its proper place.

NOTE: T.D. or a well trained assistant should supervise storage and order of items to be brought in for new set. Anyone with brawn can tote and fetch.

(j) Pull rug or ground cloth, strip it of tacks and staples, roll.

(k) Sweep stage.

NOTE: Sprinkling stage with water before sweeping tones down the dust problem.

(l) Go for food.

NOTE: Some producers have food delivered; others require workers to bring their own lunch boxes. Whatever the procedure, some provision must be made for those workers who must stay the night. It is wise to include this time-consuming errand in regular strike-night assignments.

(4) If legs and borders have been used, the following chores must also be assigned to crew members.
  (a) Lower battens.
  (b) Remove legs, fold.
  (c) Remove borders, fold.
  (d) Remove drops, fold or roll.
  (e) Raise battens.
  (f) Tote and fetch.
  (g) Store.

C—Recognize the fact that local patrons, ushers, and friends can be useful on strike night *only* if they, too, are assigned specific jobs. f, g, h, k of (3) and b, c, d, f of (4) are useful assignments for occasional workers.

D—Designate approximate deadline for completion of chores.

NOTE: The simple fact is that almost any set can be struck in an hour (complicated ones may take two). Prolonged strike nights are for dilettantes.

E—Send workers home as their tasks are completed.
  (1) Give early calls to those who retire early.
  (2) Set morning duties before they leave or, if this is impossible, tell them to whom they are to report and at what time.

F—Chalk new set on bare stage or see that scene designer does so.

G—Turn the bare stage and the crew over to the scene designer and/or technical director.

H—Assist them if necessary—go home and rest if it isn't.

14 Organize final strike of season.

A—Follow above rule for strike.

B—Check with every production department head to see that all scenery, props, costumes, sound equipment are:
   (1) Labeled and stored properly, or:
   (2) Returned to their rightful owners.

C—See that stage and back stage areas are left clean and in a safe condition.

D—Lock stage door, and back stage windows.

E—Turn key over to management.

F—Turn in final expense account.

15 In carrying out steps 1 through 14, never appear harassed, doubtful, apologetic, belligerent, or put-upon. A stage manager must not only run things smoothly, but impart confidence that it will be so.

CHAPTER 29

The Star

The star is the performer whose name will bring paying customers into the box office, if it be known that he is appearing in a particular production. He must:

1 Allow (indeed, insist) that his name and photograph be publicized.

NOTE: This "name" may have been made by a series of fine performances, one excellent or perfectly cast performance; or some curious event such as winning a tennis tournament or a wrestling match, or a beauty contest; marrying or divorcing a celebrity; being the son or daughter of a well-known star or politician. It may be the result of some super-colossal press agentry or even some fantastic surgery. How the name was made has nothing to do with the validity of stardom. With the longevity, worthiness, or respectability of stardom, yes; but with the power of a star, no.

2 Follow whichever he chooses from a long, long list of contradictory rules which have been made for stars. Herein are some of the more prevalent ones.

A—Know how to pick a vehicle.

B—Hire a good press agent.

C—Always give top-notch performances.

D—Have an excellent supporting cast.

E—Have a dull supporting cast; never anyone

who is brilliant enough (or stupid enough) to steal a scene.

- F—Appear glamorous at all times.
- G—Keep private life private.
- H—Hide nothing from the press.
- I—Stay home and take care of the health.
- J—Be seen often in elite, but publicized places.
- K—Remember that dignity becomes a celebrity.
- L—Be the life of the party.
- M—Be a kind, generous, and decent person.
- N—Be ruthless.
- O—Follow the pattern set up by his own particular star-maker.
- P—Be himself.

3 Follow the rule for the cast (see Chapter 6).

NOTE: Ah, how pleasant! But by no means necessary or even expected of a star. If however, the star does follow the rules, he will undoubtedly demand it of others in the cast. If he doesn't follow them, let it be said here and now that the others had better.

4 Know that when his name no longer brings people into the box office, he is no longer a star—no matter how fine a performer he is, no matter how fine a person. There are always new stars waiting in the wings of some little theatre or in some casting agent's office who are ready, willing, and yes, even able to take his place.

CHAPTER 30

The Technical Director

The technical director is the person who is responsible for executing the set (or sets) according to the specifications of the scene designer. He must:

1 Accept responsibility for the care of his shop and equipment.

    A—Check supplies on hand (in collaboration with scene designer, if possible) before the season starts.

    (1) Check his stock pile for size and condition and list:
- (a) Flats.
- (b) Platforms.
- (c) Stair units.
- (d) Door units.
- (e) Window units.
- (f) Columns, pedestals, balustrades, railings, etc.
- (g) Ceiling.

    (2) Check his tool supply.

    (a) List additional tools which he knows will be necessary for building the sets.

    (b) List additional tools which will be helpful to him throughout the season.

    (3) Check his hardware supply, i.e., nails, screws, hinges, staples, electric plugs, L

irons, etc. List items and amounts needed.

(4) Check his paint supply including pigments, whiting, glue, wheat paste, brushes, rollers, mixing cans, hose for washing flats, heater, etc.

    (a) Determine additional colors needed.

    (b) List supplies needed.

(5) Check lumber supply. List lumber needed for immediate use.

(6) Check fabric supply, i.e., muslin, canvas, velour, floor covering. List (in so far as possible) the materials needed for the season.

B—Order needed supplies.

(1) Find out the available local sources for obtaining *all* needed supplies.

(2) Find out approximate costs of all above supplies.

(3) Submit lists of all above supplies, including costs, to business manager or producer for approval.

(4) Order immediately upon approval.

    (a) Order in large amounts.

    (b) Order from most reasonable source.

    (c) Never wait until the cupboard is bare.

    (d) Never wait for an emergency.

NOTE: This almost always leads to the use of more expensive and less satisfactory substitutes.

    (e) Avoid (in so far as it is possible) waiting until long-distance phone calls, air-express shipments, telegrams, frenzied trips and other frantic measures are necessary.

Handbook for Theatrical Apprentices 165

        (f) Accept the fact that occasional frantic or emergency methods are inevitable; be prepared to deal with them calmly (or unfrantically, so to speak).

    (5) Keep account of all pre-season expenditures.

        (a) Turn them over to business manager before first opening night.

        (b) Keep a copy.

NOTE: If opening night turns out to be one of those frantic occasions (and that is likely) take time out the following day (no matter what) to list expenditures and turn them over to the business manager.

    C—Organize shop so that there is a *definite* place for everything when it is not in use.

    For example:

    (1) A large board with drawings of each tool, and hooks (or nails) for hanging, so that a missing tool is noticed immediately.

    (2) Either small drawers or rows of No. 10 cans labeled with sizes for nails, screws, cleats, corrugated fasteners, hinges, etc.

    (3) Hooks or clamps so that items such as brooms, rakes, dust-pans, etc., can be hung up (or at least kept stationary).

    (4) Labeled cans with covers for scene paints, glue, whiting, wheat paste (dry place!).

    (5) Large board for paint brushes [as in (1)].

    (6) Special shelf or large box for empty paint cans.

    (7) Special shelf for other paint.

    (8) Scene dock for flats, door frames, win-

dow units, headers, etc.—to be stacked so that they are easily accessible and not destructive to each other.

(9) Ditto for solid pieces such as stair units, platforms, pillars, etc.

(10) Stock piles for lumber according to size.

D—Make it absolutely clear to all assistants that everything has its place when not in use.

NOTE: Nothing short of a fainting spell is an acceptable excuse for not putting tools away at the end of the day, and each item should be put away immediately following use.

(1) Insist that paint brushes be washed out thoroughly and put away after each use.

(2) Insist that paint cans be washed out and put away after a particular color has been completed for that show.

NOTE: Nothing smells worse than stale scene paint, with the possible exception of burnt glue.

(3) Insist that no one leaves heat on under glue. Never burn blue. Just never. No further comment.

(4) See that power equipment is turned off when not in use.

(5) Never allow novices to use power equipment unless supervised.

NOTE: The T.D. must be the sole judge as to who is capable of using power equipment.

(6) Explain his system for stacking flats and other scenery when it is not in use.

(7) Insist that his own system is followed —even if another system is better. (T.D. alone may change the system.)

(8) Post basic instructions for care and placement of tools, equipment, scenery, etc.

NOTE: Leave no loophole for the usual comments—"Oh, I didn't know *that!*" "Nobody told *me* that!" "How was I supposed to know that!"

(9) Keep work area clean.

2 Assign jobs to technical assistants.

NOTE: This is probably the most difficult part of the technical director's job—especially when his assistants consist of a group of apprentices who know little about the technical aspects of the theatre, and frequently care less. Most of them are primarily interested in dreaming of carrying off opening night in a blaze of glory due to the sudden demise of the star. Anyway, here are some helpful hints which can save much time in the dawdling field and the what-can-I-do-now department.

A—Divide chores into groups:

(1) Unskilled, such as clean-up, sorting nails, sorting lumber, scrubbing flats.

(2) Semi-skilled, such as pulling flats according to size, measuring and marking lumber (T.D. must *write* measurements and type of lumber to be used). Planing or sanding down lumber, cutting cardboard, covering platforms with burlap or carpeting, putting on a base coat of paint, stretching and stapling muslin to flat frame.

(3) Skilled, such as putting a flat together, building stairs or platforms according to plan, using papier-mache for simple forms, upholstering simple furniture, stenciling.

(4) Trained assistant, such as dutchmaning (looks simple but more sets have been ruined by faulty dutchmen than any other one factor!), hinging doors so that they

hang properly, building more complex set units, mixing paint, spattering, rag-rolling, and other painting techniques.

(5) Expert—executing tasks which are too difficult for any of the other groups and usually must be handled by the T.D. himself, or by the scene designer.

B—Be specific in making assignments.

(1) Take time to explain a new job to an assistant before leaving him on his own.

For example: Never say, "Go sort the lumber." Rather say, "See this lumber? Stack all pieces over six feet long in this pile. All under six feet, but over three feet in this pile; all under three feet, but over eighteen inches in this pile, and put the rest in the trash barrel."

(2) Set deadline for completion of each task.

(3) Never overload a new apprentice with tasks which seem insurmountable.

(4) On the other hand, never make his whole day's assignment one that can be completed in 10 or 15 minutes.

(5) Be sure that one particular assistant (each week) is responsible for checking to see that tools are in their proper place and that the shop is left tidy at the end of each day.

C—Consider whole season when planning assignments.

(1) State working hours in accordance with stage manager.

NOTE: Be reasonable. Healthy, alert assistants accomplish more and last longer than tired, disgruntled ones.

(2) Post a list of basic and consistent jobs which must often be neglected during hours of stress, but which may be accomplished during off-moments and will insure some degree of future tranquility, i.e., at least lessen the hours of stress for the next show.

For example: Strip and sort lumber, wash and mend flats, straighten drawers, clean paint cans.

(3) Make a list of set pieces for future shows which can be completed and stored until needed, thus avoiding absolute chaos for the more complicated show. (Co-operation of the scene designer is obviously necessary for this listing.)

(4) Ask assistants to mark off and initial items in (2) and (3) as they are completed.

(5) Realize that his patience and training early in the season will lighten his burden as the season progresses.

    (a) Assign progressively difficult tasks according to the growing ability of assistants.

    (b) Give less detailed instructions according to the growing knowledge of assistants.

NOTE: Toward the end of the season, the T.D. may be able to say to certain assistants, "Sort the lumber when you get a chance." The assistant may even answer, "I did." It's a great day!

    D—Remember at all times that no matter who has been assigned what, the final responsibility for a smooth-running shop (or yard, as the case may be) and well-constructed sets are his own.

(1) Check progress of each assignment daily.

(2) Give further instructions if necessary.

(3) Assign additional workers to job if necessary.

(4) Give personal help if necessary.

3 Meet with scene designer no later than the day of the first rehearsal.

A—Check the renderings carefully.

B—Clear up any uncertainties that may arise.

C—If he demands the impossible according to the time, equipment, and help available, settle on a substitute then and there.

D—Be honest with scene designer and himself in discussing the above; never just wait until it is time to put the set up and then "just not have" a part of it.

4 Check supplies for executing the new set immediately following the meeting with the scene designer.

A—Pull flats and other set pieces already available.

B—List items that must be built from scratch.

C—Pull lumber already on hand for building.

D—Order all new lumber that will be needed immediately.

E—Check other supplies for building; make sure he has an ample supply of the proper-sized nails, screws, hinges, staples, etc.

F—Order special materials needed, i.e., chicken wire, burlap, newspapers, newel posts, or whatever immediately, if scene designer has not done so.

G—Check paints; order special colors immediately if scene designer has not done so.

H—Keep accounts of every cent spent.

I—Turn accounts over to business manager weekly.

5 Construct the set with the help of assistants—see 2 above—and according to the specifications of the scene designer.

NOTE: One reason for the failure or harassment of many T.D.'s is that they think their job begins here. This would be true of a master carpenter if the T.D. is lucky enough (i.e., with a large company) to have one as an assistant. In any case the time saved in organizing 1, 2, 3, and 4 are certainly well worth the effort. Indeed 5 and 6 cannot be accomplished with any degree of efficiency without such organization.

    A—Make sure construction is sufficiently sturdy.

        (1) Measure. Rule of thumb is no good.

        (2) Make practical units safe.

        (3) Make allowances for untouched set pieces.

        (4) Make allowances for pieces which must be dismantled on strike night and nail or screw accordingly.

    B—Think of every possible detail that can be completed in advance and have it completed.

    Examples:

    Knobs on doors.

    Banisters on stairs.

    Frames on door flats.

    Hardware for drapes on window units.

    Basic painting completed.

    C—Paint as early in the week as possible—especially if the painting must be done outdoors.

(1) Never assume that bad weather will improve or good weather remain constant.

(2) Always mix enough paint of a given color to complete painting in that color. It is almost impossible to exactly match paint.

(3) Leave nothing to be done after set is up which can conceivably be accomplished in advance.

D—Store completed units in safe dry place, and in an order that will make them easily removable from shop to stage.

6 Put up the set.

A—Make definite assignments to assistants in advance.

(1) Follow rules set up in 2 above.

(2) Co-ordinate "set-up" assignments with strike assignments of stage manager.

B—Dismiss each assistant when his assignment is completed.

(1) Never promote the glamour of the up-all-night-strike.

(2) Permit a bare minimum of sitting around. When a man is no longer useful, send him home.

C—Make sure that the set is secure.

D—On the other hand remember that the next strike night is bound to come.

(1) Use two-headed nails.

(2) Use stage braces.

(3) Never use seven nails when 2 are sufficient.

(4) Use staples rather than tacks when safe.

E—Make sure that all practical units *work before tech rehearsal*.

Examples:
Doors open and close properly.
Step units are nailed down.
Exit stair units are in place.
Backing is up.
Light switches exist.
Banisters are securely on stairs.
That there are no loose boards, protruding nails, slippery floors, etc.

NOTE: All of the above are absolutely essential to a smooth opening performance. They are possible only if all rules in "5" have been followed faithfully.

 F—Dress set before dress rehearsal at latest, before tech when practical.

NOTE: The actual dressing of the set is the responsibility of the prop man and the scene designer; however, the T.D. must have the set ready far enough in advance to give them ample time for dressing.

 G—Take final notes as given by director and/or scene designer during tech and dress rehearsals.

 H—Make final corrections and repairs.

 I—Make set repairs during run of the play according to instructions of stage manager.

7 Become a member of the crew when necessary. (Stage manager is always judge of the necessity.) See CHAPTER 10 on THE CREW.

8 Assist with strike according to stage manager's plan.

CHAPTER 31

The Usher

The usher is one of the persons responsible for seeing that each member of the audience is seated properly (i.e., in the seat designated on his ticket stub) and for giving him a program. The *head* usher, sometimes called house manager, must:

1 Organize the ushers.

    A—See that there is a sufficient number of ushers available for each performance.

    B—Explain the seating arrangement to each usher.

    C—Set time for ushers to arrive before each performance, allowing time before doors open to:

        (1) See that all seats are turned up.

        (2) Adjust slip-covers (if used).

        (3) Dust seats (if necessary).

        (4) Acquire programs and put them in easily accessible places.

        (5) Complete extra-curricular chats with other ushers.

    D—Explain proper dress to each usher.

    E—Assign each usher to a definite section of the theatre.

    F—Assign at least one person to stay on duty throughout each performance. His duties will be to:

(1) Turn up seats after the audience has left.

(2) Note any defects in seats, i.e., numbers missing, screws loose, slip-covers loose, etc.

(3) Report defects to person designated by management—usually head usher or production stage manager.

(4) Close windows.

(5) Put programs away.

G—Keep telephone numbers of all ushers handy.

2 Take tickets.

NOTE: The head usher may designate another person to take tickets; if so, he must explain the following clearly:

A—Take tickets from each person or group of persons as they enter.

B—Tear the tickets in half.

C—Give one half of the ticket to the customer (so the usher will know where to seat him).

D—Put the other half of the ticket into a container provided for this purpose immediately.

E—When all tickets are in for each performance, remove the ticket stubs from the container, put them in an envelope, close it, and turn the envelope into the box-office.

NOTE: This is very important for balancing the books and for tax purposes.

3 Personally check seats weekly and report defects to management.

4 Report reasonable customer complaints to management.

Each usher must:

1 Assume a professional attitude even if he is a volunteer worker.

A—Designate dates that he will serve.
B—Give his telephone number to the head usher.
C—Give adequate notice to head usher if he is unable to serve at any time.
D—Dress neatly and according to rules of management.
E—Memorize seating arrangement.
F—Report on time for each performance. (See "C" under head usher.)
G—Be courteous to everyone.
H—Seat audience quickly as possible.
I—Give programs to each member of the audience.

NOTE: All programs for a small group may be given to one member of the group.

J—Seat late-comers quietly.
K—Never chat or giggle with other ushers after the doors open, either before or during performance.

CHAPTER 32

The Variety Worker

The variety worker (for want of a better term) is a person who assumes responsibility for various odd jobs which, alas, have no title, seem unrelated to the theatre, but exist in every theatre, nevertheless.

As these jobs vary so drastically from company to company it is almost impossible to set down hard-and-fast rules. Still, there are about ten commandments which apply to enough members of enough companies in enough situations to warrant mention. A variety worker must:

1 Recognize the existence of odd jobs and accept his fair share of responsibility for them.
2 Never accept full responsibility for a job unless he is fairly sure he knows how to handle it.
3 Never allow first-week exuberance and eagerness-to-please to trap him into excessive odd chores, which may cause neglect of his regular job during the height of the season.
4 Never "just stop" doing odd jobs without turning responsibility over to another person through proper authorities.
5 Always keep financial accounts of jobs requiring the handling of money. Collect the money weekly. Never wait until the end of the season.
6 Never drive off in company vehicles without permission from proper authorities.

7 Never feel obligated to lend his privately-owned car to "just anyone who asks."
8 Never allow privately-owned car to become a company vehicle unless agreeable financial arrangements have been made in advance.
9 Never lend clothes or other personal property unless it is really agreeable.
10 Never expect to use other people's personal property unless he is willing to lend his own.

Various odd jobs which arise fairly frequently are:

1 Going for food.
2 Organizing company parties.
3 Attending social functions given by patrons.
4 Driving members of the company to social functions.
5 Driving members of the company to meals.
6 Picking up and delivering personal laundry for members of the company.
7 Personal shopping for members of the company.
8 Picking up mail.
9 Furnishing props or costumes from personal belongings.
10 Cuing actors.

CHAPTER 33

Yourself

You, yourself, are the one person in the whole wide world who is responsible for you.

As time goes on, you may acquire fame and fortune, personal managers and press agents, family and friends. None of these can ever alter this fact. Philosophers from Aristotle to Abby Lane have expounded this one truth. I won't even pretend to add to their theories. I will try to form some clear-cut rules which may help you to "be true to thine own self," as the saying goes, through a production season.

1 Take care of your health.

    A—Eat properly. Don't expect to get by on sandwiches, soft drinks, and candy bars.

    B—Sleep when it is possible, because there will be times when it isn't. Don't kid yourself on this one.

    C—Don't fret. Either work on the problem or forget about it.

    D—Keep clean. Bathe, brush your teeth, wash your hair, wear reasonably clean clothes, regularly.

    E—Dress up at least once a week. This is especially good for the morale of the technical crew.

    F—Relax occasionally. Use your free hours for things that relax you. If it's "the thing" to go for a beer when you would rather go for a swim, go for a swim. Vice versa and et cetera.

G—Keep your sense of humor.

NOTE: Summer stock especially is serious business, plain hard work and maybe even an art form, but you'll never last a season if you don't find the funny side of it too.

2 Mind your manners.

No further comment, except this: Politeness, even solicitude, with very important people does not constitute good manners when accompanied by rudeness to those of lesser status. By the same token, extreme kindness to fellow workers, waiters, janitors, visitors, etc. does not lessen your obligation to be reasonably polite to the VIPs.

For example: If anyone invites you to a party, accept graciously or send regrets. Say "thank you" for parties, gifts, or special favors, even if the giver has millions and merely treats you to a coke. In other words, a caste system does exist in the theatre, but it does not apply to common courtesy.

3 Consider your reputation.

A—Don't lose sight of the fact that the whole wide world of theatre is very small.

B—Don't walk out on a job without adequate notice. (Adequate notice being sufficient time for your particular company to find a replacement.) You will be put down as an unreliable, untrustworthy, unfair, unfit, and unpleasant nobody, to say the very least.

C—Don't blame your incompetence on other members of the company. Everybody will know sooner or later, anyway, and you will be put down as a constant complainer.

Handbook for Theatrical Apprentices 181

D—Never demand or even suggest that another person be fired unless you can:

(1) Prove that the person in question is a real detriment to the company.

(2) Be absolutely sure that a "personality clash" is not involved.

(3) Take over his job in addition to your own, or:

(4) Recommend a better person who is available at the same wages (unless, of course, you are personally willing to pay the wage difference).

You will be put down as a busybody.

E—Don't neglect your work for your social life. You will be put down as a dilettante.

F—Don't brag about your past efforts unless your present ones can measure up. You will be put down as a braggart and a bore.

G—Don't say you will do things that you have no intention of doing or that you are incapable of doing. You will be put down as a liar.

H—Don't go around with a chip on your shoulder. You will be put down as a-person-who-goes-around-with-a-chip-on-his-shoulder.

I—Always work at your own maximum ability, no matter what "the others" are doing. You will be put down for future reference.

4 Use your imagination.

Without this last rule, all the others become null and void. Every job in the theatre is a creative one. Your success or failure will depend upon the imagination, personality, and drive you use to augment your efficiency.

6 RMS RIV VU
BOB RANDALL

(Little Theatre) Comedy
4 Men, 4 Women, Interior

A vacant apartment with a river view is open for inspection by prospective tenants, and among them are a man and a woman who have never met before. They are the last to leave and, when they get ready to depart, they find that the door is locked and they are shut in. Since they are attractive young people, they find each other interesting and the fact that both are happily married adds to their delight of mutual, yet obviously separate interests.

"... a Broadway comedy of fun and class, as cheerful as a rising souffle. A sprightly, happy comedy of charm and humor. Two people playing out a very vital game of love, an attractive fantasy with a precious tincture of truth to it."— *N.Y. Times.*
"... perfectly charming entertainment, sexy, romantic and funny."—*Women's Wear Daily.*

WHO KILLED SANTA CLAUS?
TERENCE FEELY

(All Groups) Thriller
6 Men, 2 Women, Interior

Barbara Love is a popular television 'auntie'. It is Christmas, and a number of men connected with her are coming to a party. Her secretary, Connie, is also there. Before they arrive she is threatened by a disguised voice on her Ansaphone, and is sent a grotesque 'murdered' doll in a coffin, wearing a dress resembling one of her own. She calls the police, and a handsome detective arrives. Shortly afterwards her guests follow. It becomes apparent that one of those guests is planning to kill her. Or is it the strange young man who turns up unexpectedly, claiming to belong to the publicity department, but unknown to any of the others?

"... is a thriller with heaps of suspense, surprises, and nattily cleaver turns and twists ... Mr. Feeley is technically highly skilled in the artificial range of operations, and his dialogue is brilliantly effective."—*The Stage. London.*

THE SEA HORSE
EDWARD J. MOORE

(Little Theatre) Drama
1 Man, 1 Woman, Interior

It is a play that is, by turns, tender, ribald, funny and suspenseful. Audiences everywhere will take it to their hearts because it is touched with humanity and illuminates with glowing sympathy the complexities of a man-woman relationship. Set in a West Coast waterfront bar, the play is about Harry Bales, a seaman, who, when on shore leave, usually heads for "The Sea Horse," the bar run by Gertrude Blum, the heavy, unsentimental proprietor. Their relationship is purely physical and, as the play begins, they have never confided their private yearnings to each other. But this time Harry has returned with a dream: to buy a charter fishing boat and to have a son by Gertrude. She, in her turn, has made her life one of hard work, by day, and nocturnal love-making; she has encased her heart behind a facade of toughness, utterly devoid of sentimentality, because of a failed marriage. Irwin's play consists in the ritual of "dance" courtship by Harry of Gertrude, as these two outwardly abrasive characters fight, make up, fight again, spin dreams, deflate them, make love and reveal their long locked-up secrets.

"A burst of brilliance!"—*N.Y. Post.* "I was touched close to tears!"—*Village Voice.* "A must! An incredible love story. A beautiful play!"—*Newhouse Newspapers.* "A major new playwright!"—*Variety.*

THE AU PAIR MAN
HUGH LEONARD

(Little Theatre) Comedy
1 Man, 1 Woman, Interior

The play concerns a rough Irish bill collector named Hartigan, who becomes a love slave and companion to an English lady named Elizabeth, who lives in a cluttered London town house, which looks more like a museum for a British Empire on which the sun has long set. Even the door bell chimes out the national anthem. Hartigan is immediately conscripted into her service in return for which she agrees to teach him how to be a gentleman rather after the fashion of a reverse Pygmalion. The play is a wild one, and is really the neverending battle between England and Ireland. Produced to critical acclaim at Lincoln Center's Vivian Beaumont Theatre.

A Breeze from The Gulf

MART CROWLEY

(Little Theatre) Drama

The author of "The Boys in the Band" takes us on a journey back to a small Mississippi town to watch a 15-year-old boy suffer through adolescence to adulthood and success as a writer. His mother is a frilly southern doll who has nothing to fall back on when her beauty fades. She develops headaches and other physical problems, while the asthmatic son turns to dolls and toys at an age when other boys are turning to sports. The traveling father becomes withdrawn, takes to drink; and mother takes to drugs to kill the pain of the remembrances of things past. She eventually ends in an asylum, and the father in his fumbling way tries to tell the son to live the life he must.

"The boy is plunged into a world of suffering he didn't create. . . . One of the most electrifying plays I've seen in the past few years . . . Scenes boil and hiss . . . The dialogue goes straight to the heart." Reed, Sunday News.

ECHOES

N. RICHARD NASH

(All Groups) Drama
2 Men, 1 Woman, Interior

A young man and woman build a low-keyed paradise of happiness within an asylum, only to have it shattered by the intrusion of the outside world. The two characters search, at times agonizingly to determine the difference between illusion and reality. The effort is lightened at times by moments of shared love and "pretend" games, like decorating Christmas trees that are not really there. The theme of love, vulnerable to the surveillances of the asylum, and the ministrations of the psychiatrist, (a non-speaking part) seems as fragile in the constrained setting as it often is in the outside world.

". . . even with the tragic, sombre theme there is a note of hope and possible release and the situations presented specifically also have universal applications to give it strong effect . . . intellectual, but charged with emotion."—Reed.

VERONICA'S ROOM
IRA LEVIN
(Little Theatre) Mystery
2 Men, 2 Women, Interior

VERONICA'S ROOM is, in the words of one reviewer, "a chew-up-your-fingernails thriller-chiller" in which "reality and fantasy are entwined in a totally absorbing spider web of who's-doing-what-to-whom." The heroine of the play is 20-year-old Susan Kerner, a Boston University student who, while dining in a restaurant with Larry Eastwood, a young lawyer, is accosted by a charming elderly Irish couple, Maureen and John Mackey (played on Broadway by Eileen Heckart and Arthur Kennedy). These two are overwhelmed by Susan's almost identical resemblance to Veronica Brabissant, a long-dead daughter of the family for whom they work. Susan and Larry accompany the Mackeys to the Brabissant mansion to see a picture of Veronica, and there, in Veronica's room, which has been preserved as a shrine to her memory, Susan is induced to impersonate Veronica for a few minutes in order to solace the only surviving Brabissant, Veronica's addled sister who lives in the past and believes that Veronica is alive and angry with her. "Just say you're not angry with her," Mrs. Mackey instructs Susan. "It'll be such a blessin' for her!" But once Susan is dressed in Veronica's clothes, and Larry has been escorted downstairs by the Mackeys, Susan finds herself locked in the room and locked in the role of Veronica. Or is she really Veronica, in the year 1935, pretending to be an imaginary Susan?

> The play's twists and turns are, in the words of another critic, "like finding yourself trapped in someone else's nightmare," and "the climax is as jarring as it is surprising." "Neat and elegant thriller."—*Village Voice*.

MY FAT FRIEND
CHARLES LAURENCE
(Little Theatre) Comedy
3 Men, 1 Woman, Interior

Vicky, who runs a bookshop in Hampstead, is a heavyweight. Inevitably she suffers, good-humouredly enough, the slings and arrows of the two characters who share the flat over the shop; a somewhat glum Scottish youth who works in an au pair capacity, and her lodger, a not-so-young homosexual. When a customer—a handsome bronzed man of thirty—seems attracted to her she resolves she will slim by hook or by crook. Aided by her two friends, hard exercise, diet and a graph, she manages to reduce to a stream-lined version of her former self—only to find that it was her rotundity that attracted the handsome book-buyer in the first place. When, on his return, he finds himself confronted by a sylph his disappointment is only too apparent. The newly slim Vicky is left alone once more, to be consoled (up to a point) by her effeminate lodger.

> "My fat Friend is abundant with laughs."—*Times Newsmagazine*. "If you want to laugh go."—*WCBS-TV*.

PROMENADE, ALL!
DAVID V. ROBISON

(Little Theatre) Comedy
3 Men, 1 Woman, Interior

Four actors play four successive generations of the same family, as their business grows from manufacturing buttons to a conglomerate of international proportions (in the U.S. their perfume will be called Belle Nuit; but in Paris, Enchanted Evening). The Broadway cast included Richard Backus, Anne Jackson, Eli Wallach and Hume Cronyn. Miss Jackson performed as either mother or grandmother, as called for; and Cronyn and Wallach alternated as fathers and grandfathers; with Backus playing all the roles of youth. There are some excellent cameos to perform, such as the puritanical mother reading the Bible to her son without realizing the sexual innuendoes; or the 90-year-old patriarch who is agreeable to trying an experiment in sexology but is afraid of a heart attack.

"So likeable; jolly and splendidly performed."—*N.Y. Daily News.* "The author has the ability to write amusing lines, and there are many of them."—*N.Y. Post.* "Gives strong, lively actors a chance for some healthy exercise. And what a time they have at it!"—*CBS-TV.*

ACCOMMODATIONS
NICK HALL

(Little Theatre) Comedy
2 Men, 2 Women, Interior

Lee Schallert, housewife, feeling she may be missing out on something, leaves her husband, Bob, and her suburban home and moves into a two-room Greenwich Village apartment with two roommates. One roommate, Pat, is an aspiring actress, never out of characters or costumes, but, through an agency mix up, the other roommate is a serious, young, graduate student—male. The ensuing complications make a hysterical evening.

"An amusing study of marital and human relations . . . a gem . . . It ranks as one of the funniest ever staged."—*Labor Herald.* "The audience at Limestone Valley Dinner Theater laughed at 'Accommodations' until it hurt."—*News American.* "Superior theater, frivolous, perhaps, but nonetheless superior. It is light comedy at its best."—*The Sun, Baltimore.*

THE GOOD DOCTOR
NEIL SIMON
(All Groups) Comedy
2 Men, 3 Women. Various settings.

With Christopher Plummer in the role of the Writer, we are introduced to a composite of Neil Simon and Anton Chekhov, from whose short stories Simon adapted the capital vignettes of this collection. Frances Sternhagen played, among other parts, that of a harridan who storms a bank and upbraids the manager for his gout and lack of money. A father takes his son to a house where he will be initiated into the mysteries of sex, only to relent at the last moment, and leave the boy more perplexed than ever. In another sketch a crafty seducer goes to work on a wedded woman, only to realize that the woman has been in command from the first overture. Let us not forget the classic tale of a man who offers to drown himself for three rubles. The stories are droll, the portraits affectionate, the humor infectious, and the fun unending.

"As smoothly polished a piece of work as we're likely to see all season."—*N.Y. Daily News.* "A great deal of warmth and humor —vaudevillian humor—in his retelling of these Chekhovian tales."—*Newhouse Newspapers.* "There is much fun here . . . Mr. Simon's comic fancy is admirable."—*N.Y. Times.*

(Music available. Write for particulars.)

The Prisoner of Second Avenue
NEIL SIMON
(All Groups) Comedy
2 Men, 4 Women, Interior

Mel is a well-paid executive of a fancy New York company which has suddenly hit the skids and started to pare the payroll. Anxiety doesn't help; Mel, too, gets the ax. His wife takes a job to tide them over, then she too is sacked. As if this weren't enough, Mel is fighting a losing battle with the very environs of life. Polluted air is killing everything that grows on his terrace; the walls of the high-rise apartment are paper-thin, so that the private lives of a pair of German stewardesses next door are open books to him; the apartment is burgled; and his psychiatrist dies with $23,000 of his money. Mel does the only thing left for him to do: he has a nervous breakdown. It is on recovery that we come to esteem him all the more. For Mel and his wife and people like them have the resilience, the grit to survive.

"Now all this, mind you, is presented primarily in humorous terms."—*N.Y. Daily News.* "A gift for taking a grave subject and, without losing sight of its basic seriousness, treating it with hearty but sympathetic humor . . . A talent for writing a wonderfully funny line . . . full of humor and intelligence . . . Fine fun."—*N.Y. Post.* "Creates an atmosphere of casual cataclysm, and everyday urban purgatory of copelessness from which laughter seems to be released like vapor from the city's manholes."—*Time.*

A COMMUNITY OF TWO

JEROME CHODOROV

(All Groups) Comedy

4 Men, 3 Women, Interior

Winner of a Tony Award for "Wonderful Town." Co-author of "My Sister Eileen," "Junior Miss," "Anniversary Waltz." This is a charming off-beat comedy about Alix Carpenter, a fortyish divorceè of one month who has been locked out of her own apartment and is rescued by her thrice-divorced neighbor across the hall, Michael Jardeen. During the course of the two hours in which it takes to play out the events of the evening, we meet Alix's ex-husband, a stuffed shirt from Wall Street, her son, who has run away from prep school with his girl, heading for New Mexico and a commune, Michael's current girl friend, Olga, a lady anthropologist just back from Lapland, and Mr. Greenberg, a philosopher-locksmith. All take part in the hilarious doings during a blizzard that rages outside the building and effects everybody's lives. But most of all, and especially, we get to know the eccentric Michael Jardeen, and the confused and charming Alix Carpenter, who discover that love might easily happen, even on a landing, in the course of a couple of hours of high-stress living.

"Thoroughly delightful comedy."—*St. Louis-Post Dispatch*. "A joy."—*Cleveland Plain Dealer*. "Skillful fun by Jerome Chodorov."—*Toronto Globe Star*.

ROMAN CONQUEST

JOHN PATRICK

(All Groups) Comedy

One set—3 Women, 6 Men

The romantic love story of two American girls living in the romantic city of Rome in a romantic garret at the foot of the famous Spanish steps. One of the world's richest young women takes her less fortunate girl friend to Italy to hide unknown and escape notoriety while she attempts to discover if she has any talent as an artist—free of position and prestige. Their misadventures with language and people supply a delightful evening of pure entertainment. Remember the movies "Three Coins in the Fountain" and "Love Is A Many Splendored Thing"? This new comedy is in the same vein by the same Pulitzer Prize winning playwright.

COUNT DRACULA
TED TILLER

(All Groups) Mystery comedy

7 Men, 2 Women. Interior with Small Inset
1930 Costumes (optional)

Based on Bram Stoker's 19th Century novel, "Dracula." This is a new, witty version of the classic story of a suave vampire whose passion is sinking his teeth into the throats of beautiful young women. Mina, his latest victim, is the ward of Dr. Seward in whose provincial insane asylum the terrifying action transpires. Her fiance arrives from London, worried over her strange inertia and trance-like state. Equally concerned is Professor Van Helsing, specialist in rare maladies, who senses the supernatural at work. Added trouble comes from Sybil, Dr. Sewards demented, sherry-tippling sister and from Renfield, a schizophrenic inmate in league with the vampire. But how to trap this ghoul who can transform himself into a bat, materialize from fog, dissolve in mist? There are many surprising but uncomplicated stage effects, mysterious disappearances, secret panels, howling wolves, bats that fly over the audience, an unexpected murder, and magic tricks which include Dracula's vanishing in full view of the spectators.

Despite much gore, ". . . the play abounds with funny lines. There is nothing in it but entertainment."—*Springfield, Mass. News.*

FRANKENSTEIN
TIM KELLY

(All Groups)

4 Men, 4 Women, Interior

Victor Frankenstein, a brilliant young scientist, returns to his chateau on the shores of Lake Geneva to escape some terrible pursuer. No one can shake free the dark secret that terrifies him. Not his mother, nor his fiancee Elizabeth, nor his best friend, Henry Clerval. Even the pleading of a gypsy girl accused of murdering Victor's younger brother falls on deaf ears, for Victor has brought into being a "Creature" made from bits and pieces of the dead! The Creature tracks Victor to his sanctuary to demand a bride to share its loneliness—one as wretched as the Creature itself. Against his better judgment, Victor agrees and soon the household is invaded by murder, despair and terror! The play opens on the wedding night of Victor and Elizabeth, the very time the Creature has sworn to kill the scientist for destroying its intended mate, and ends, weeks later, in a horrific climax of dramatic suspense! In between there is enough macabre humor to relieve the mounting tension. Perhaps the truest adaptation of Mary Shelley's classic yet. Simple to stage and a guaranteed audience pleaser.

Outstanding One-Act Plays for Tournament Use

- RECOGNITION SCENE FROM ANASTASIA
- APOLLO OF BELLAC
- EMPEROR'S NIGHTINGALE
- STILL STANDS THE HOUSE
- INCOME TAX, THE
- HEATHEN PIONEER
- PORTRAIT OF NELSON HOLIDAY, JR.
- SHERIFF, THE
- SHIRKERS, THE
- TOUCH OF FANCY
- HEAT LIGHTNING
- THIS WAY TO HEAVEN
- WHEN THE FIRE DIES
- ADAM'S RIB HURTS
- FOREVER JUDY
- UGLY DUCKLING, THE
- PERIOD HOUSE
- RIDERS TO THE SEA
- FRIGHT
- FUMED OAK
- SISTERS MC INTOSH
- FROM FIVE TO FIVE-THIRTY
- BISHOP'S CANDLESTICKS, THE
- PERFECT GENTLEMAN, THE

The Overcoat

Children's Play
BY NICOLAI GOGOL
Adapted by Tom Lanter and Frank S. Torok

5 males, 3 females, minimum.
Minimal scenery. Period costumes.

Gogol himself is a principal character, spinning his story from nothing but the rags of a tattered old overcoat, which is pitifully unsuited for the rigors of the Saint Petersburg winters. He creates Akaky Akakievich—a poor dedicated copy clerk who becomes obsessed with the idea of having a new overcoat—and then the author steps into the story to become the Chief Clerk, Akaky's boss, Petrovich, the tailor, and then the Very Important Person who refuses to help the shivering Akaky when the precious garment is stolen. Fun, mime, fantasy, alphabet and overcoat dreams, a sympathetic ghost, simple but ingenious scenery—and the appropriately soaring music of Tchaikovsky—all combine to create a superbly funny yet moving theatre piece. A great success when first produced at the Yale Repertory Theatre. Winner in the Wilmette Children's Theatre Playwrighting Contest in 1974.

How the Chicken Hawk Won the West

(All Groups.) Children's Play.
BY GIFFORD W. WINGATE
Music by Mitch Kendrick

7 males, 5 females. Exterior, unit set.

A chicken hawk, unhappy about the fact that he is seldom visited at his home in the aviary of a zoo, attempts to improve his public image. Chief among the devices he uses to lure unsuspecting visitors to his compound is a dramatic rendering of "The Winning of the West," in which he features himself in a variety of scenes as "The Lone Chicken Hawk"; as the inventor of "The Chicken Hawk Express"; as "Kung Chicken Hawk," builder of the nation's first railroad; as "William Allen Chicken Hawk," editor of the first frontier newspaper; and as "Judge Roy Bird—Law West of the Pecos." A group of children and the adults who brought them are induced to play the supporting parts. History takes a beating, but so does the ego of the Chicken Hawk, who accepts at the end an identity closer to reality. The play is simple to stage and can be toured easily. Music is published in the script.

The Overcoat

Children's Play
BY NICOLAI GOGOL
Adapted by Tom Lanter and Frank S. Torok

**5 males, 3 females, minimum.
Minimal scenery. Period costumes.**

Gogol himself is a principal character, spinning his story from nothing but the rags of a tattered old overcoat, which is pitifully unsuited for the rigors of the Saint Petersburg winters. He creates Akaky Akakievich—a poor dedicated copy clerk who becomes obsessed with the idea of having a new overcoat—and then the author steps into the story to become the Chief Clerk, Akaky's boss, Petrovich, the tailor, and then the Very Important Person who refuses to help the shivering Akaky when the precious garment is stolen. Fun, mime, fantasy, alphabet and overcoat dreams, a sympathetic ghost, simple but ingenious scenery—and the appropriately soaring music of Tchaikovsky—all combine to create a superbly funny yet moving theatre piece. A great success when first produced at the Yale Repertory Theatre. Winner in the Wilmette Children's Theatre Playwrighting Contest in 1974.

How the Chicken Hawk Won the West

(All Groups.) Children's Play.
BY GIFFORD W. WINGATE
Music by Mitch Kendrick

7 males, 5 females. Exterior, unit set.

A chicken hawk, unhappy about the fact that he is seldom visited at his home in the aviary of a zoo, attempts to improve his public image. Chief among the devices he uses to lure unsuspecting visitors to his compound is a dramatic rendering of "The Winning of the West," in which he features himself in a variety of scenes as "The Lone Chicken Hawk"; as the inventor of "The Chicken Hawk Express"; as "Kung Chicken Hawk," builder of the nation's first railroad; as "William Allen Chicken Hawk," editor of the first frontier newspaper; and as "Judge Roy Bird—Law West of the Pecos." A group of children and the adults who brought them are induced to play the supporting parts. History takes a beating, but so does the ego of the Chicken Hawk, who accepts at the end an identity closer to reality. The play is simple to stage and can be toured easily. Music is published in the script.